D0444069

CIVIC AGRICULTURE

CIVIL SOCIETY:
HISTORICAL AND CONTEMPORARY
PERSPECTIVES

Series Editors

VIRGINIA HODGKINSON
Public Policy Institute
Georgetown University

KENT E. PORTNEY
Department of Political Science
Tufts University

JOHN C. SCHNEIDER
Department of History
Tufts University

Brian O'Connell, *Civil Society: The Underpinnings of American Democracy*

Philip H. Round, *By Nature and by Custom Cursed: Transatlantic Civil Discourse and New England Cultural Production, 1620–1660*

Bob Edwards, Michael W. Foley, and Mario Diani, eds. *Beyond Tocqueville: Civil Society and the Social Capital Debate in Comparative Perspective*

Ken Thomson, *From Neighborhood to Nation: The Democratic Foundations of Civil Society*

Henry Milner, *Civic Literacy: How Informed Citizens Make Democracy Work*

Virginia A. Hodgkinson and Michael W. Foley, eds., *The Civil Society Reader*

Thomas A. Lyson, *Civic Agriculture: Reconnecting Farm, Food, and Community*

Civic Agriculture

RECONNECTING FARM, FOOD, AND COMMUNITY

Thomas A. Lyson

TUFTS UNIVERSITY PRESS

Medford, Massachusetts

Published by University Press of New England
Hanover and London

TUFTS UNIVERSITY PRESS

Published by University Press of New England,

One Court Street, Lebanon, NH 03766

www.upne.com

© 2004 by Tufts University

Printed in the United States of America

5 4 3 2 1

All rights reserved. No part of this book may be reproduced in any form or by any electronic or mechanical means, including storage and retrieval systems, without permission in writing from the publisher, except by a reviewer, who may quote brief passages in a review. Members of educational institutions and organizations wishing to photocopy any of the work for classroom use, or authors and publishers who would like to obtain permission for any of the material in the work, should contact Permissions, University Press of New England, One Court Street, Lebanon, NH 03766.

CIP data appear at the back of the book.

FOR MY WIFE,
Loretta Carrillo

AND MY DAUGHTERS,
Mercedes Carrillo Lyson and Helena Carrillo Lyson

CONTENTS

[vii]

CONTENTS

TABLES

ACKNOWLEDGMENTS

The path to civic agriculture began in 1988 when I became the director of Cornell's Farming Alternatives Program (FAP). Although the program was established during the farm crisis of the mid-1980s to help New York farmers "ease out" of dairying and into "alternative enterprises," its mission changed in the 1990s from assisting individual farmers to working with groups of farmers and community development practitioners to promote a more sustainable agriculture and food system in the state. Sustainability became the focus of much of my research and writing during the 1990s. And it was during this period that the emergence of a new form of agriculture and food production became visible. Farmers' markets were springing up everywhere around New York State. Small-scale food processors appeared on the radar screen. Community and school gardens began dotting the landscape. And organic farmers were organizing into networks to more effectively market their products.

For a while we called these emerging forms of agriculture and food production the "New Agriculture." They were new in many important and significant ways, not the least of which was that they had strong ties to community and the environment. But there was another "New Agriculture" on the block. The nation's agricultural biotechnology companies were proclaiming that genetically modified organisms (GMOs) were going to serve as the foundation of a "New Agriculture" that would feed the world. If the biotechnology corporations had appropriated the term "New Agriculture" for their purposes, what did we have?

The new forms of production, processing, and distribution that we were tracking clearly had a connection to place and people. They were more than just a set of new production techniques. They were "civic." And so in 1999 I coined the term "civic agriculture" in a paper I delivered at the annual meetings of the Rural Sociological Society.

I owe thanks to many individuals for their support, assistance, and encouragement. My colleagues in the Community, Food, and Agriculture Program (formerly the Farming Alternatives Program), Joanna Green, Heidi Mouillessaux-Kunzman, Duncan Hilchey, and Gretchen Gilbert, have integrated many of the civic concepts into their work and put a human face on civic agriculture.

Over the past fifteen years Gil Gillespie and I have worked on several large agriculture and food system projects. The results generated from these projects have provided grist for this book. Jennifer Wilkins in the Division of Nutritional Sciences at Cornell showed me the connection of my work to community nutrition. Phil McMichael's work on global food systems served as a very useful counterpoint to my interest in the local. Jeff Sobal's conceptual work on the agriculture and food system helped me situate my work in a broader systems context.

I have had the good fortune to work with many talented graduate students at Cornell. I have learned from all of them. Melanie DuPuis showed me how state-level agricultural policy preserved family farming in some places while leading to industrialization in other areas. Clare Hinrichs looked at how farming, family, and community are bound together. Rick Welsh delved into the survival strategies of family farmers. Beth Barham compared the sustainable agriculture movement in France with that in the United States. Bob Torres showed how denominations of origin can nurture local agriculture development. Robin Kreider has shown how informal organic marketing standards become formalized. And Matt Hoffman has tested the civic agriculture model in Vermont.

Outside of Cornell, Doug Harper's work on "changing works" among dairy farmers in the Northeast showed me how community and farming could be brought together. My understanding of the civic community benefited from my collaborations with Charlie Tolbert, Mike Irwin, and Troy Blanchard. Gail Feenstra and Mike Hamm read my manuscript with a critical eye. Their comments and suggestions are much appreciated.

A project of this sort unfolds over many years. The Cornell University Agricultural Experiment Station helped fund my civic agriculture research. A special thanks goes to Ronnie Coffman and Dan Decker, who supported not only my work but that of my colleagues in the Community, Food, and Agriculture Program.

Finally, my wife, Loretta, and daughters Mercedes and Helena showed infinite patience and good humor throughout this project.

CIVIC AGRICULTURE

CHAPTER I

Introduction

Community Agriculture and Local Food Systems

Civic Agriculture

While the American food and agriculture system follows a decades-old path of industrialization and globalization, a counter trend toward localizing some agriculture and food production has appeared. I call this rebirth of locally based agriculture and food production *civic agriculture,* because these activities are tightly linked to a community's social and economic development. The organizational manifestations of civic agriculture such as farmers' markets, community gardens, and community-supported agriculture are not monitored by most federal or state agencies, so what we know about this new form of agriculture and food production comes mainly from the civic agriculture community itself.

Civic agriculture does not currently represent an economic challenge to the conventional agriculture and food industry, and it is unlikely to pose a challenge anytime soon. However, it does include some innovative ways to produce, process, and distribute food. And it represents a sustainable alternative to the socially, economically, and environmentally destructive practices that have come to be associated with conventional agriculture. The term "civic agriculture" references the emergence and growth of community-based agriculture and food production activities that not only meet consumer demands for fresh, safe, and locally produced foods but create jobs, encourage entrepreneurship, and strengthen community identity. Civic agriculture brings together production and consumption activities within communities and offers consumers real alternatives to the commodities produced, processed, and marketed by large agribusiness firms.

Farming and Food Today

America's agriculture and food have changed dramatically over the past several decades. Smaller, family-labor farms have declined substantially in number as larger, increasingly industrial-like operations have become the main source of food and fiber. Technologically sophisticated and highly standardized production techniques have penetrated most segments of the farm and food economy, and advances in plant and animal sciences have resulted in substantial increases in production. These advances have become linked tightly to a narrow range of bulk products.[1]

In the past, farmers produced bulk commodities that they sold to brokers, wholesalers, and other middlemen, who, in turn, directed these commodities to food processors or retailers. The consumer was presented with a fairly standard set of products on supermarket shelves. Today, a case is being made—mostly by large food processors and retailers—that consumers are no longer satisfied with the homogeneous fare they received in the past. They are now "demanding" food products tailored to their individual tastes and preferences. "Have it your way" at Burger King and "Think outside the bun" from Taco Bell are part of a push by the food industry to create "you food," food products that are tailored to your life. Fast-food outlets sit at the end of supply chains that stretch around the world. The shelves in modern grocery stores and supermarkets are stocked with products that have been produced and processed thousands of miles away.

As U.S. agriculture has modernized and industrialized it has also regionalized. Farmers in areas that were once characterized by diverse agricultural activities have been driven to exploit their "comparative advantage." Producers in the Great Lakes states, for example, have been able to establish and maintain a niche in dairy production. Producers in the Plains states have been able to raise hogs cheaper than farmers elsewhere, while farmers in California and several other Sunbelt states have used subsidized water and a favorable growing climate to become the leading producers of fresh fruits and vegetables. More recently, agricultural regionalization within the United States has given way to global regionalization as producers from all over the world participate in an emerging "global" agricultural marketplace.[2]

The emerging configuration of agriculture and food production in the United States and the world has been guided by an economic development paradigm grounded in neoclassical/market-based economics. For farm operators, the "production function," which describes the economic sustainability of agriculture in terms of the optimal balancing of land, labor, and capital, has long served as an important tool for farm management. Throughout most of this century, farm management professionals have emphasized substituting capital, in the form of machinery, chemicals, and other off-farm inputs, for land and labor.[3]

At another level, the neoclassical paradigm treats agriculture as just another industry, not unlike manufacturing or mining, and calls for the introduction of labor-saving, mass-production techniques throughout the production process. The guiding principles are that agricultural production should be concentrated into fewer units to capture economies of scale, machinery should be substituted for labor whenever possible, and the remaining jobs should be routinized to the point that workers within occupational categories become "interchangeable."

Beyond the farm gate, the processing sector of the food industry has also been shaped by neoclassical precepts. To capture the benefits associated with economies of scale, many small food processors have been forced to expand, merge with larger operations, or go out of business. During the latter half of the twentieth century, large, multinational food processors became dominant in the food sector of the American economy as they gained control over large segments of the food system. Today, the ten largest multinational corporations account for over 60 percent of the retail purchases of food in the United States.[4] Mass-production manufacturers and mass-market retailers provide abundant quantities of relatively inexpensive, standardized products. While these giant food corporations are still forming, their growth and development has shaped local agriculture and food systems in every region of the country.

Today, no region of the United States can be said to be even substantially self-sufficient in food production. Consumers depend heavily on imported products that can be produced only in climates and soils outside their regions. In many areas of the country, there is little or no locally produced food in commercial channels. The peri-urban areas around many large American cities have the soils and climate needed to produce a broad array of food products. Historically, these areas were sources of fresh fruits, vegetables, and dairy and meat products. Fruit and vegetables from nearby "truck farms" were a regular staple during the summer and fall in many urban food economies. The industrialization of agriculture coupled with a policy of cheap energy, however, made it possible to move food great distances at little cost. At the same time, places that have little or no local resources to produce food have burst forth as America's fastest-growing cities. These cities are tethered to food pipelines that extend around the globe.[5]

The relationships between large-scale, regionally concentrated agricultural producers, national and multinational food processors and distributors, and the structure of local food systems are complex, geographically dispersed, and heavily influenced by policy. For example, as the agricultural landscape of California changed in the early part of the twentieth century to accommodate large-scale, corporately controlled fruit and vegetable farms, the number of fruit and vegetable farms in the Northeast declined. Between 1910 and 1950 the value of small fruits and berries and tree fruits increased from $20.1 million to $106 million in California, a 421 percent increase, while in New York the value of small fruits and berries and tree fruits increased only 25 percent from $20.9 million in 1910 to only $26.2 million in 1950. At the same time, the food system in the Northeast was transformed from a more locally interdependent system of production and consumption to a more globally oriented system where production was uncoupled from consumption. These changes have impacts that go far beyond the agricultural sector. The character and structure of communities are dramatically altered by these trends.

A global system of food production, one that is controlled by large national and multinational corporations, has already begun to refashion how and, more importantly, where food is produced. Driving the global/industrial system of farming is the continual search by agribusiness firms for areas of low-cost production. In a global system of food production, labor and capital flow to places where maximum profits can be extracted.

A Place for Civic Agriculture

Communities can buffer and shelter themselves from the global food system only if they develop the needed infrastructure, maintain a sufficient farmland base, and provide enough technical expertise so that local farmers and processors can successfully compete in the local marketplace against the highly industrialized, internationally organized corporate food system. There is accumulating evidence that a relocalization of agriculture and food systems is taking place in regions that have been hit hard by global competition. It is not surprising that Massachusetts, New York, and other states in the Northeast are in the vanguard of the relocalization efforts. Large-scale, industrial farming has largely bypassed this region, and consumers there must rely on food produced elsewhere.

Although the nature and range of agricultural products found in most American communities are shaped by the decisions made by large multinational firms, important environmental, social, political, and economic reasons justify the re-emergence of a smaller-scale, more locally controlled food system. A new *civic agriculture* is emerging and taking hold in every region of the country. Community-supported agriculture (CSA), farmer's markets, specialized agricultural districts, alternative food stores, and consumer cooperatives represent important manifestations of the movement toward a civic agriculture. These new organizational forms have the potential to nurture local economic development, maintain diversity and quality in products, and provide forums where producers and consumers can come together to solidify bonds of local identity and solidarity. By rebuilding the linkages between farmers and consumers wherever possible, communities throughout the United States will establish a foundation for a more socially and environmentally integrated food system.

Plan of the Book

In the next chapters I examine the global and local dimensions of America's agriculture and food system today. I begin with an overview of how agricultural producers in the United States moved from a local, self-sufficient system of food production, processing, and distribution to an industrially organized, globally managed system. I then explore corporate control of the food system. Following this, I identify a set of trends and possibilities that suggest that a relocalization of production and processing may be occurring throughout the United States. I outline theoretical and organizational dimensions of this emerging civic agriculture. The book concludes with some thoughts about the future of the American food system.

CHAPTER 2

From Subsistence to Production

How American Agriculture Was Made Modern

Agriculture and Rural Life

Less than one hundred years ago most rural households in the United States sustained themselves by farming. While some agricultural products were sold for money on the open market, others were produced solely for household consumption or for bartering with neighbors. All family members, including husbands, wives, and children, contributed their labor to the economic maintenance and survival of the household. While there was a well-established division of labor along gender and age lines in many farm households, there was not a well-articulated and formalized occupational structure within most rural areas. In this social and economic context, the household, the community, and the economy were tightly bound up with one another. The local economy was not something that could be isolated from society. Rather the economy was embedded in the social relations of the farm household and the rural community.

Local communities served as trade and service centers for the farming population. Rural communities also served as places that nurtured participation in civic and social affairs, and as such they could be viewed as nodes that anchored people to place. And, as most commentators have noted, schools played a key role in solidifying and defining community boundaries.

Two early rural sociologists, John H. Kolb and Edmund de S. Brunner, describe the settlement of the Middle West and Far West this way. "Individual farms were settled by families who went out to get land and to seek their fortunes. They settled in groups on adjoining farms and were bound together by such ties as kinship, common nationality, the same education, social, or religious purposes." Within the rural communities, "Mutual aid, exchange of work, building bees, social affairs, schools and churches soon became the organized ways of these groups."[1]

In rural households, men, women, and children engaged in a wide range of productive enterprises. On the farm, they grew crops, raised animals, cleared land, built and repaired machinery, engaged in home-based manufacturing, and maintained the farmstead. A typical farm in the United States in 1870, for example, was very small by today's standards. Most farm families survived on less than seventy-five acres. Indeed, in 1870 less than one-third of the nation's farms had one hundred acres of improved cropland. The typical family farm produced a wide range of commodities, including dairy products (e.g., cheese, butter, milk), tobacco, fresh fruits, and vegetables. Gross sales, though crudely estimated in the nineteenth century, averaged about $1,200 a year.[2] Much of what was produced was not sold on the market but rather was bartered for goods and services in the local community or else used for home consumption.

Household-based productive activities in rural areas are more difficult to ascertain, since no systematic data were ever collected in this area. However, we know from historical accounts that the members of farm households produced a broad range of goods for their own consumption including clothes, furniture, and housewares. Labor exchanges and bartering were also an embedded feature of the economic life in rural communities.

Doug Harper describes the social nature of "changing works" this way:

> The principle of changing works was that farmers informally organized themselves . . . to share labor. There were many forms of changing works in different regions of the country, depending on the duration of the work which needed to be done, the density of farms in a region, and the technology at a given stage of agricultural development. . . . In [Illinois in the 1920s] . . . farmers grew several crops, including large fields of grain. Each July a group of farmers in a neighborhood collectively rented a thresher, which they moved from one farm to another. Given the size of the grain fields in the region, it took a thresher crew up to two weeks to do the crop on a single farm. While harvesting the crop, the crew stayed on the farm. Thus, the farm women fed up to twenty people a day for ten to fourteen days in a row. . . . [3]

Some manufacturing of durable and nondurable goods in rural areas also took place outside of farm households. Many rural communities had metalworking enterprises, woodworking shops, and related activities. The Census of 1870, for instance, shows that in the three most rural northern New England states, Vermont, New Hampshire, and Maine, there were 12,162 manufacturing establishments. On average, these places employed fewer than ten workers. Sawmills, blacksmith shops, flour and gristmills, wagon-making enterprises, and leather-related industries, such as saddle/harness shops and shoe factories, predominated.

Much of this economic activity was organized around small, skilled, artisan shops. Artisan shops are places that employ a handful of workers and do not use water or steam power in the production process but rather rely on hand- or foot-powered machinery. Factories that relied on water or steam power were virtually unknown in the United States in the early 1800s and this type of economic organization did not penetrate rural areas of the country to any great extent until after the Civil War. In 1810, for example, only 2.8 percent of the American workforce could be found in such factories.[4] By 1870, however, 58 percent of the factories in northern New England were waterpowered and another 6.7 percent were powered by steam.

Nonfarm rural households shared many of the characteristics of households engaged in agricultural production. Nonfarm work roles, though a bit less embedded in household structures, were nevertheless well integrated into the local community. A set of distinct occupational titles that reflected a rigid and formalized division of labor was of little use in most rural areas. In fact, the U.S. Census acknowledged the ambiguity in attempting to classify rural nonfarm workers into existing occupational schemes in the 1870 Census.

> As communities advance in industrial character, functions become separated, and distinct occupations become recognized. . . . [However, in] many of the communities of the land it is difficult to draw distinctions much finer than those between the agricultural, the mining, the mechanical, and the commercial pursuit of professions. Indeed, even this is not practicable, since it is a matter of notoriety that . . . the occupations of carpenter and farmer, or blacksmith and farmer, or farmer and fisherman, are frequently united in one person. In large and more prosperous communities a clear separation

between such incongruous occupations takes place; yet still, the carpenter, for instance, in nine out of ten counties in the United States, performs a half a dozen functions which, in cities, are recognized as belonging to distinct trades.[5]

The idea of "economic embeddedness" is clearly important for understanding how agriculture and food production were organized in the 1800s, and it has considerable value in helping understand the relocalization of agriculture that is taking place in America today as well. We know from a small, but growing, body of research in rural sociology and allied disciplines that there are many different ways rural people "make a living" and provide for their material needs today. Working for wages in a job and buying goods and services in the marketplace are the ways most Americans typically think about the contemporary economy. Indeed, from the perspective of neoclassical economics, the modern economy is one in which families and workers engage almost entirely in formal market transactions bereft of any social or cultural meaning. Beyond the marketplace of the economists, however, lies an economic terrain rich in substance and meaning. Households and communities provide the context in which economic transactions transpire. The "market," in neoclassical terms, is but one of many venues for "economic" activity.[6]

The Emergence of Modern Economic Forms

In the early 1800s, economy and society were woven of the same cloth in rural America. Agricultural production and manufacturing were organized along very similar social lines. This was the era of protoindustrialization and small-scale family farming. Labor in both manufacturing and agriculture was relatively undifferentiated, and there were few special-ized work roles. The broad range of labor skills held by one individual and the relative smallness of the production enter-prises has been labeled "craft production" by many modern-day observers.[7]

As a system of economic production, craft-based manufac-turing and agricultural enterprises produced a diverse array of goods for local markets. We would call this "customized pro-duction" today. The geographic landscape of rural America, then, consisted of identifiable conglomerations of economic activities that met local needs. Regional and national mar-kets, such as they existed in the early part of the nineteenth century, were small relative to the aggregate demand of the local markets.

An economic revolution occurred in the mid-1800s in the United States with the advent of mass-production techniques in manufacturing. The system of craft production that had dominated the economic landscape for centuries began to give way to relatively large-scale ensembles of production ac-tivities organized in one central location. As Michael Piore and Charles Sabel note in *The Second Industrial Divide,* "The visionaries of mass production foresaw a world of ever more automated factories, run by fewer and ever less skilled work-ers."[8] While it has been assumed that advances in technology were the driving force behind mass production, recent histor-ical scholarship has begun to show that at least initially the rise of the factory system was due not to superior forms of technical efficiency but rather to a capitalist philosophy of "so many hands, so much money." That is, the amount of profit was tied directly and almost exclusively to the amount of labor employed. For example, the best-known way for a bicy-cle manufacturer to increase his profits would be to add more bicycle makers to his factory. In strictly economic terms, early mass production increased gross profits but did not necessarily raise the rate of profit. In a study of early factories in Indianapolis, Robert Robinson and Carl Briggs found "that firms with large numbers of workers and large investments in capital had no efficiency advantage over firms with small work forces and limited capital investments. There were *no economies of scale* in any industry in 1850, 1870, or 1880. Nor did the introduction of water- or steam-powered technologies—the defining characteristics of factories—result in greater output. . . . "(italics added).[9]

Over time, of course, technological improvements in manufacturing processes emerged. Water, steam, and later electrical power supplanted human labor in production. Manufacturing output became standardized and routinized. At the same time, efficient transportation networks opened up regional and national markets to local manufacturers. Mass markets articulated with mass production. Workers in factories that adopted mass-production techniques became increasingly differentiated along task lines as capital in the form of machinery was substituted for labor in many industries. Michael Piore and Charles Sabel make the point well: "By World War I . . . industry after industry had come under the domination of giant firms using specialized equipment to turn out previously unimagined numbers of standardized goods, at prices that local producers could not meet."[10] The culmination of this transformation from craft production to mass production was most evident in the assembly lines of the Ford Motor Company. In fact, the system of mass-production manufacturing that is organized around assembly-line forms of social organization has taken on the name "Fordism" in the contemporary economic organization literature.[11]

Early Agricultural Development

Agriculture was not immune to the organizational changes experienced by the manufacturing sector. The organization and operation of modern American farms bears little resemblance to the way agriculture was organized in the mid 1800s. The forerunners of "scientific agriculture" can be traced to the lyceum and Chautauqua movements of the 1820 to 1840 era. During this period information about the latest advances in agriculture and farming was passed along through community-based educational efforts. Farm households came together in their local neighborhoods and communities to share information, to exchange ideas, and to learn new techniques in the local lyceums and through the traveling chautauquas.[12]

The organizing impetus behind scientific agriculture in the United States was the Morrill Act of 1862. This act established the land-grant system of colleges and universities that has become the model of modern agriculture throughout the world. The formation of the land grant system was the first organized and coordinated attempt to bring "rationality" and standardization to agricultural production. The Morrill Act set in motion the introduction of scientific principles and applied science to agriculture. It represented the genesis of the "American Way of Farming."[13]

The mission of the land-grant colleges and universities was expanded in 1887 when the Hatch Act was passed. This piece of legislation created an agricultural experiment station in each state; their mission was to support basic and applied research in the agricultural sciences. In 1914, the Smith-Lever Act established a mechanism to fund a nationally organized system of outreach. In theory, the Cooperative Extension

Service was to deliver to farms and farm households the knowledge and techniques developed at the land-grant universities.

Unlike manufacturing, which adopted assembly-line techniques in the early part of the twentieth century, it was clear to most agricultural scientists that the system of relatively small-scale, family-based farming that existed at that time could not be organized along mass-production lines. There was too much idle time for labor in the production process; hence the division of labor along specialized task lines was difficult, if not impossible. Furthermore, there were simply too many different and interrelated tasks involved in producing food and fiber to allow much headway to be made in dividing labor among those tasks. Finally, there was incredible variability in conditions across farms in terms of soils, climate, and other environmental variables. This environmental variability meant that farming enterprises took different forms in different places. Even within the same state or within the same county, the variability across farms could be tremendous. Unlike factories, which could standardize the production process, farms could not standardize the environmental conditions under which they produced food.[14]

Despite these caveats, the community of agricultural scientists at the U.S. Department of Agriculture (USDA) and on the campuses of America's land-grant universities, along with agribusiness leaders, assumed that productivity and output could be increased by standardizing and rationalizing the production process. The pressure to increase productivity to meet the needs of a rapidly expanding mass market for agricultural commodities was the driving force behind the introduction of "modern farming methods." The land-grant system rose to the challenge by devising new production techniques, new equipment, and new and improved crop varieties that continually boosted agricultural productivity.

However, the advocates of scientific agriculture were faced with a "clientele" of farmers who were rooted in tradition, suspicious of "book-learned" techniques, and averse to risk.[15] If agriculture was going to modernize and keep pace with advances in the manufacturing sector, it needed an organizational model or blueprint that could be presented to farmers as a rationale for accepting (buying into) the new ways of producing food. If American farmers were to break out of the mold of producing food in ways that were not markedly different from the ways of their ancestors, they needed some assurance that they would not go broke in the process.

The answer to the farmer's need for guidance was emerging in the field of economics. Throughout the early 1900s, the first generation of agricultural economists worked to devise a standard set of criteria that would allow farm enterprises to be evaluated along the same lines as manufacturing enterprises.

At the Seventh Annual Meeting of the American Farm Management Association in 1916, the vice president of the organization, H. W. Jeffers from Plainsboro, New Jersey, put it this way: "What is needed is a clear cut, standard farm plan for each type of farming in each region so that a person starting farming in a new region, or the farmer who is not making the farm pay, or the extension worker who is conducting demonstrations can make use of such a plan by modifying it to meet the local conditions."[16]

In working through this endeavor, economists found it was necessary to decontextualize the farm enterprise from the community and household settings in which it was embedded. That is, they found it necessary to remove the household and community context from the economic function of production agriculture. This was done by building a model of agriculture that rested squarely on individual decision making related to the four economic factors of production: land, labor, capital,

and management/entrepreneurship. The sine qua non of farming to economists was to provide the information needed to
educate farm operators about how to balance the four factors
to maximize both output and profitability. Social relations in
the household and community, along with nonmarket transactions that might impinge upon the "rational calculations" of
the farm operator, were deemed "externalities" and largely ignored as unimportant to agricultural production.[17]

From the very beginning, this organizational blueprint for
agriculture was set up to industrialize farming by mimicking
the model of mass-production manufacturing. As early as
1913, farm management specialists were guiding agriculture
into the mainstream economy. Charles Brand, speaking to the
annual meeting of American Farm Management Association,
noted:

> Agriculture is a business industry, and as such is merely one
> part of the great business structure of the country. If farming is
> to continue profitable . . . we must in the next decade or two
> give the same attention to the business side of farming that we
> have in the past two decades to the producing side.[18]

When set in motion, the neoclassical "production function" model of farming was designed to increase agricultural
productivity by substituting capital in the form of machinery,
chemicals, and other purchased inputs and management inputs for labor and land. The goal was to increase agricultural
production on less land and by using less labor. In this model
the farm manager is the prime mover behind the whole operation. It is the farmer who orchestrates how the factors of production will be deployed on his farm.

Over the past hundred years, land-grant universities, the
USDA, and more recently large agribusiness firms have thrown

farmers wave upon wave of new technologies on the path to industrialization. Willard Cochrane saw these new technologies as a "technological treadmill" that the farmers had to hew to if they expected to survive. Farmers who slipped off the treadmill were often branded as "laggards" and held in disdain by the efficiency-oriented agricultural community. It is easy to see why so many farmers failed to keep pace on the treadmill. As craft production gave way to mass production in the manufacturing sector and "scientific management" wrested control of the shop floor out of the hands of workers, American farmers were yoked to a set of technologies that promised to make production easier and more efficient—but at a cost. That cost was that fewer and fewer producers would be needed.[19]

Three Agricultural Revolutions

The industrialization of American agriculture was marked by three major technological "revolutions." The first, the "mechanical revolution," dates from the early 1900s, when tractors and associated farm machinery were introduced to the farm. In 1910 fewer than 1 percent of the nation's 6.4 million farms had a tractor. By 1950, there were over 3.4 million tractors on 5.4 million farms. The introduction of the tractor allowed a farmer to work more land and consequently reduced the need for farm labor. Not surprisingly, between 1910 and 1950, the number of workers on American farms decreased by 26.8 percent. Farmland, on the other hand, increased by 31.8 percent during this period, in part to meet the food needs of a rapidly growing population.

The second revolutionary change occurred shortly after the end of World War II, when the use of synthetic fertilizers and pesticides skyrocketed on American farms. The "chemical revolution" was propelled by the conversion of bomb-making and other war-related chemical plants to agrochemical plants. As Richard Merrill notes, ". . . World War II can be thought of as the instigator of an agricultural revolution." The production of DDT, 2,4-D, and organic phosphates increased dramatically after the war. By the 1970s, there were "over 100 industrial plants producing about 1,000 pesticide chemicals variously combined in over 50,000 registered pesticides."[20]

Between 1945 and 1980, the use of synthetic fertilizers increased by 715 percent. One effect of the increased use of agrochemicals was to increase crop yields. This meant that less land was needed to meet the food and fiber needs of the country. In the thirty years between 1950 and 1980, 175 million acres of farmland were taken out of production. During this same period, crop yields increased by 75.4 percent.

Table 2.1 shows the relationships among numbers of farms, farm acreage, tractors, and amounts of fertilizer used on U.S. farms. Both the number of farms and the amount of farmland under production were high prior to the start of the two agricultural revolutions. However, as the number of tractors began to increase, the number of farms decreased. Likewise, as fertilizer use increased after World War II, both the number of farms and the amount of farmland in production decreased. Both mechanization and the use of chemical inputs contributed to farm consolidation as smaller holdings were combined into larger, more efficient units of production.

In the 1980s, a third agricultural revolution began to sweep across American farms—the "biotechnology revolution." Biotechnology, which includes genetic engineering and recombinant DNA technology, is increasing the output of both plant and animal agriculture. Unlike the mechanical and the chemical revolutions, biotechnology promises to have significant

Table 2.1. Changes in the Structure of Agriculture from 1910 to 1997: Farms, Acres, Tractors, and Fertilizer

Year	Farms	Acres (1,000s)	Tractors	Fertilizer (tons)
1910	6,361,502	878,798	6,000	5,547
1920	6,448,343	955,884	540,488	7,176
1930	6,288,648	986,771	920,000	8,425
1940	6,096,799	1,060,852	1,545,000	8,656
1950	5,382,162	1,158,566	3,394,000	20,991
1960	3,962,520	1,175,646	4,770,000	25,400
1970	2,954,200	1,102,769	4,619,000	38,292
1980	2,432,510	1,038,855	4,775,000	50,368
1990	2,140,420	987,420	4,305,000	47,700
1997	2,191,360	953,500	3,936,000	55,000

Sources: Agricultural Statistics, various years; U.S. Census of Agriculture, 1997.

impacts on nearly all aspects of agriculture and food production. It is still too early to tell how the biotechnology revolution will affect the use of land and labor. However, most observers believe that it is likely to result in a greater concentration of production on fewer, but larger farms. Less land and less labor will be required to meet our food and fiber needs.[21]

Today, the traditional farm management blueprint for agriculture is so ingrained in the minds of farmers, policy makers, and agricultural professionals that it has become "the world as given" to them. Most people associated with agriculture in the United States assume that staying on the agricultural treadmill and producing more food with less land and less labor is the *only* way agriculture can or should be organized. And, in fact, this is the model of production that is being exported to developing nations as the "American way of farming."

By adopting, without question, a strictly economic view of production agriculture, the stage was set for the development of a market-oriented, economically focused system of farming that could be uncoupled from communities and households. If agriculture could be viewed in the same manner as manufacturing, then there was no reason not to expect a trend toward mass production, standardization, and homogenization of agricultural commodities. And, indeed, over the past hundred years this is exactly the path farming has taken.

The Social Construction of Modern Economic Categories

Mass production, whether in manufacturing or agriculture, has given rise to a mode of economic analysis anchored to "free markets" as mechanisms that order both production and consumption. This mode of analysis is based on constructs that have little connection to noneconomic social forms. The terms "industry" and "occupation," for example, are disembodied economic concepts that are most amenable to a strictly economic form of analysis.[22] They have been "constructed" apart from any social context (household, community, etc.) to which they might be naturally linked.

In the realm of farming, agricultural economists have focused virtually all their attention on the "economically efficient" production and marketing of selected "standard" commodities. Not all commodities have attracted the same amount of attention by the agricultural establishment. Those commodities that can be "mass-produced" in accordance with the precepts put forth by the neoclassical production function and that articulate with standardized mass markets have garnered most of the attention. Thus, for example, there are detailed econometric analyses of the production practices for all the major market-oriented commodities such as corn, wheat, and soybeans, and considerable research time and money are devoted to fine-tuning these models.

Nonstandard varieties or commodities that have not achieved "economies of scale" because they are too embedded in household or community relations to get an "economically unencumbered" reading, have been largely ignored by the conventional agricultural community. Maple sugar, cedar oil, and various direct-marketed fruits and vegetables, for instance, are commodities that have historically been and continue to be important livelihood activities for many farm households and farm communities in the Northeast. However, these commodities have been overlooked by mainstream agricultural economics and treated in the academic literature as either "marginal" or "peripheral" farm enterprises. From a neoclassical, market perspective the income generated from maple, cedar, and direct marketing is small vis-à-vis the receipts from standardized, bulk commodities like milk, corn, or soybeans; yet cedar, maple, and direct-marketing activities help sustain, and in many instances totally support, many rural households, even though these activities cannot be easily quantified or categorized. The production of maple sugar and cedar oil and the direct marketing of fruits and vegetables are deeply embedded in the social fabric of the region and households of the Northeast.

In short, the picture of rural life presented to us by neoclassical economics, whether of its agriculture or nonagricultural aspects, is framed in terms of well-defined markets and constructed categories of land, labor, capital, and management, which are organized to fit the production function. These categories typically do not articulate with the community and household relations that can and do structure everyday economic activities. Although economists using such models could ignore the community contexts and social relations that are part and parcel of local economic life, they could not make them disappear. The embeddedness of economic life, ignored by mainstream economics for the past hundred years, surfaced about three decades ago in the writings of development specialists who observed that, despite very low labor-force participation rates in many Third World countries, as measured by official statistics, most able-bodied men and women were engaged in all sorts of "economic" activities.

Civic Economy, Economic Embeddedness, and the Informal Economy

The term "informal economy" was coined in the early 1970s to refer to the earning and spending patterns of the urban subproletariat in the Third World.[23] It is not surprising that informal and semiformal economic arrangements became most apparent in developing countries, since it is in the Third World that the "seams" of the neoclassical viewpoint are most evident. During the 1950s and 1960s, the most widely accepted path to economic modernization for less-developed countries was to adopt the Western model of industrialization. This model posited that the best engines of economic growth for less-developed countries were open/free markets fed by large-scale, capital-intensive, mass-production enterprises run by multinational corporations. Agricultural economies could be transformed into modern, industrial economies by rationalizing the agricultural sector, moving people off of the land and into cities, and establishing and nurturing an urban-centered manufacturing export base.[24]

The spread of the Western model of market development and industrialization throughout most of the Third World during the 1950s through the 1970s was quite remarkable. However, it is important to note that the process of "modernization" was essentially a "top-down" endeavor. That is, the Western model of development was imposed on countries throughout the Third World with little regard to existing institutions and social structures. Multinational factories were simply set down in less-developed countries around the world, while large-scale, mass-market retail establishments filled with consumer goods became fixtures in Third World cities around the globe. And while a small handful of countries have benefited from this economic development strategy and have made dramatic strides toward mirroring "modern," Western-like economies (e.g., Korea, Taiwan, Singapore), many others have not seen the hoped-for results.[25]

The embedded economy is most evident in those countries that have not succeeded in developing full-blown industrial economies. In these nations, only a relatively small fraction of the laborers work for wages and provide for most of their needs through commercial market transactions. Larger segments of the population survive in a world of local capitalism that includes not only the exchange of goods, services, and labor for money but also barter, informal work arrangements, and labor exchanges. For these people, the neoclassical conception of the economy as being separate from the household or community has little meaning. The flow of money through formal market channels and the constructed categories (occupations, industries, etc.) used by economists to chart growth and change in the developing world hide a social and economic reality that is far more complex and multifaceted than the picture that is often presented in official statistics and reports.

The Civic/Embedded Economy in the United States

About twenty-five years ago, social scientists in the United States and other advanced industrial countries "discovered" a thriving civic economy in American cities.[26] Oftentimes, civic production and consumption activities are embedded in ethnic or racial enclaves. These activities not only serve as markers of economic well-being but also contribute to social, cultural, political, and environmental aspects as well.

Community and school gardens are a growing part of the civic economy of many American cities. They exist below the radar screens of most official data-gathering organizations and agencies in the United States. In New York City, for example, it is estimated that there are a thousand community gardens that operate on about three hundred acres of land. This "farmland" is used to produce fresh fruits, vegetables, flowers, herbs, and other products. No one has undertaken a comprehensive study of all of the economic, social, and environmental benefits that accrue to community gardens. However, from anecdotal evidence, we know that some of these community gardens provide fruits and vegetables to low-income neighborhoods where access to these products is limited or nonexistent. Community gardens develop "agricultural literacy" among urban residents who might otherwise have no way of learning about how their food is produced. And, as places where local residents can come together to work on a joint, mutually beneficial endeavor, community gardens foster social cohesion and neighborliness in places that are seemingly inhospitable to community formation.[27]

Like their counterparts in the Third World, however, many people in the American underclass have not been enveloped by the occupational and industrial categories used to define the formal economy. Most localities contain cadres of self-employed craftsmen and craftswomen, entrepreneurs, and individuals whose occupational and industrial profile are not easily determined. At best, their economic activities are shoehorned into existing analytical frameworks for macroaccounting purposes. The fact that their day-to-day economic life does not correspond to notions about regular employment in formal labor markets is almost always lost in the process.

While the concept of embedded economic activity, especially the informal economy, has caught the attention of Third World development specialists and urban social scientists in advanced industrial societies, the concept has been less frequently applied to rural areas in the United States.[28] This omission is understandable given that the seams of the civic economy have been covered up by the spread of Wal-Marts, Borders Books, and fast-food franchises of every stripe and by the rigid occupational and industrial categories that have been laid down by generations of economists.

If one carefully reads any of a multitude of books on farming, agriculture, or farm life that have been published over the past twenty years, however, it is clear that the richness, multidimensionality, and civic qualities of economic life in rural America never disappeared.[29] They were simply ignored or glossed over by most observers. Ethnographic accounts of production agriculture reveal a richly textured set of intertwined household, community, and economic relations. Norms of reciprocity within farming communities, for example, are evident everywhere, though they are seldom integrated into the economic calculus of the farm business. The following exchange recorded in *Waucoma Twilight*, an ethnography of a small rural village in northeastern Iowa, illustrates this point.

JEROME: I think people should work together, it should be not just one person working. That's my idea about a farmer, you know. If you got a little trouble, your neighbor comes over and helps you quick, or you go over and help him, just like a little family, the whole bunch of them a family, you know.

RITA: It's one big family.

JEROME: You know, so they all kind of work together, not just I work this now and you work that, you stay on your side of the fence and I'll stay on mine. If you kind of mix up together, you all get along better than if you don't do that.[30]

At the community level, farmers' markets, community-supported agriculture, community kitchens, and U-pick operations represent the organizational, associational, and institutional characteristics of the civic economy. Like community gardens, these enterprises bridge the economic, social, cultural, and political dimensions of community life. Their effects and benefits are not easily tallied by economists. Yet we would all be poorer for their absence.

In summary, there are many examples that illustrate the extent to which the economic terrain in rural areas is much more "textured" than the economists would have us believe. The production-driven, market-based system of conventional agriculture espoused by the U.S. Department of Agriculture and the land-grant universities is being increasingly challenged by producers and consumers who hold to a broader vision of how economic enterprises are integrated into and contribute to household and community. For example, the sustainable agriculture movement represents an attempt to embed the economics of agricultural production within an environmental, community, and household context. By giving environmental and social factors equal footing with economics, proponents of sustainable agriculture are challenging the assumption that the economic aspects of farming should be the sole driving force in dictating how our food and fiber are produced.[31]

Despite the emerging recognition that a civic economy can be found in most communities, there are powerful forces that continue to push the agriculture and food system down the path toward increased consolidation and concentration. I turn to these trends in the next chapter.

CHAPTER 3

Going Global

The Industrialization and Consolidation of Agriculture and Food Production in the United States

From Craft Production to Mass Production

Large-scale, factory-like farms account for the bulk of food and fiber produced in the United States today. The mass production of food has articulated with mass consumer markets to offer consumers relatively inexpensive, standardized products. The range of agricultural commodities produced in America has been narrowed considerably in the past hundred years to bulk commodities such as wheat, corn, soybeans, a few varieties of fruits and vegetables, and a handful of genetically similar breeds of livestock and poultry. At the same time, the "system of agriculture and food production" has taken on a new spatial pattern as well. At the beginning of the twentieth century many regions of the country were fairly self-sufficient in producing the commodities their residents consumed. Today, however, consumers depend upon many imported products that can be produced only in climates and soils outside their region or even the nation.[1]

Several long-term trends have shaped America's food and agricultural system over the past hundred years. First, farm numbers have steadily declined. In 1910 there were nearly 6.4 million farms in the United States. Today, there are fewer than 2 million. Second, production has become concentrated on a small number of very large farms. And the most highly industrialized farms are clustered together in "agricultural pockets" throughout the country. At the same time, regions of the country that at one time produced substantial amounts of agricultural products have seen farming all but disappear. Third, farms in every region of the country have become increasingly specialized, many producing only one or two commodities for the market. And fourth, with the exception of some dairy products, including fluid milk and specialty produce, the linkages between local production and local consumption have been broken for virtually all commodities. Not only are large amounts of fresh fruits and vegetables, meat, and processed dairy products being shipped great distances, but once vital local food-processing sectors have all but vanished from most regions.[2]

The Trend toward Concentration and Consolidation

The information in tables 3.1 and 3.2 illustrates some key structural changes in U.S. agriculture between 1910 and 1997. The data in these tables tell a story of a dramatic transformation of agriculture from a system that was comprised of many farm operators who produced a broad array of commodities on relatively small plots of land to a system of production in which a handful of very large-scale, specialized producers now account for the bulk of sales. For example, the average farm size in the United States increased slowly between 1910 and 1950, from 138.1 acres to 215.3 acres, but then accelerated after 1950. Today, the average farm is close to 500 acres.

Table 3.1. Farm Structure Information and Enterprise
Diversification on U.S. Farms: 1910, 1950, 1997

	1910	1950	1997
Farms (N)	6,361,500	5,382,167	1,911,859
Acres (N)	878,798,325	1,158,565,852	931,795,255
Value of products ($1,000)	8,244,920	22,052,256	196,864,649
	% of farms engaged in the enterprise		
Animal Enterprises			
Poultry	87.8	78.3	5.0
Horses	73.8	39.4	19.6
Dairy cattle	80.8	67.8	6.1
Hogs	68.4	55.9	5.7
Sheep	9.6	5.9	3.4
Plant Enterprises			
Hay (forage)	53.5	50.6	46.4
Wheat	22.9	21.3	12.7
Soybeans	*	11.2	18.5
Cotton	26.9	20.6	1.6
Potatoes	50.0	30.6	.6
All vegetables	78.1	71.0	*
Vegetables for sale	*	6.4	2.8
Apples	46.8	28.9	1.5
Oats	34.2	30.4	4.7
Corn	75.7	63.2	22.5
Pears	20.1	15.6	.4
Plums	17.6	10.6	.3
Cherries	19.6	14.8	.4
Peaches	29.0	20.5	.4

Sources: Thirteenth Census of the United States, volumes 5–7 (Agriculture); U.S.
Census of Agriculture, 1950; U.S. Census of Agriculture, 1997.
* Data not available.

Table 3.2. Concentration of Agricultural Production by Various Commodities: 1997 Census of Agriculture

	Large farms (sales >$1 million)	Total farms in category	% of all farms in category	% of sales by large farms	Average sales of large farms	Average sales of other farms
Vegetable	3,066	53,641	5.7	75.2	$2,061,612	$41,143
Fruit	3,227	85,973	3.8	58.6	$2,299,428	$63,324
Dairy	3,390	99,238	3.4	35.6	$1,996,230	$127,599
Hogs	3,748	102,106	3.7	51.7	$1,904,618	$67,776
Poultry	5,433	63,246	8.6	57.7	$2,365,663	$162,776
Corn	6,104	359,666	1.7	10.0	$310,772	$48,048
Wheat	5,825	241,334	2.4	11.4	$140,111	$26,996
Soybeans	6,021	353,566	1.7	8.6	$224,311	$41,065
All farms	25,934	1,911,859	1.36	41.7	$3,166,152	$60,847

Source: U.S. Census of Agriculture, 1997.

Large-scale producers in the United States are accounting for an ever increasing share of production. Consider that the number of America's largest farms, those with average sales of over $500,000 a year or greater, grew by over 600 percent, from 11,412, to 68,794, between 1974 and 1997. During this same period, the total number of farms dipped from 2.3 to 1.9 million.

Very large farms are more likely than smaller farms to receive government payments and to be organized as corporations. In 1997, very large farms, those generating over $500,000 a year in sales, comprised less than 3.6 percent of all farms in the country. However, they operated nearly 20 percent of the farmland and accounted for 56 percent of all farm sales.

At the top of the heap are the megafarms, those operations with annual sales of $1 million or more a year. In 1997 there were 25,934 farms in this category. These million-dollar farms represent only 1.4 percent of all U.S. farms, but they produce almost 42 percent of all farm products sold.

Many of these large-scale operations have taken on the organizational characteristics and adopted sets of production practices that mimic the mass-production model of manufacturing.[3] The guiding business principles are that production should be concentrated into fewer units to capture economies of scale, machinery should be substituted for labor whenever possible, and an advanced division of labor should replace the multiple and diverse tasks performed by the "typical" family farmer.

As American agriculture became more specialized and more highly capitalized at the farm gate, it also became more highly specialized by commodity and more regionally concentrated. In 1910, almost 90 percent of all farms raised poultry, over 80 percent had dairy cattle, about 70 percent raised hogs, and nearly 75 percent had horses. Even by 1950, significant proportions of American farmers were still engaged in these animal enterprises. However, by 1997, only 5 percent of U.S. farms reported poultry, 6 percent had dairy cattle, fewer than 6 percent raised hogs, and fewer than 20 percent had horses. Most of the horse farms, of course, sold no agricultural commodities but instead served as stables for horseback-riding urbanites and suburbanites.

Similar patterns are also evident for plant agriculture, though extreme concentration is most evident for fruits and vegetables. In 1910, almost 80 percent of American farmers grew vegetables, half of the farms grew potatoes, 46.8 percent produced apples, and around 20 percent produced other orchard fruits such as peaches, pears, plums, and cherries. As late as 1950, American farms still had a diversified portfolio of fruits, vegetables, and grains. But like animal enterprises, by 1997 the production of fruits and vegetables had become very specialized. Today, only 2.8 percent of American farmers are commercial vegetable producers, fewer than one farmer in fifty grows apples, and fewer than one in a hundred supply the country with peaches, pears, plums, or cherries.

Not only has American agriculture become more specialized over the past hundred years, but it has become amazingly concentrated. Take vegetables, for example. There were 53,641 farms that reported vegetable sales in the 1997 Census of Agriculture. But the largest 3,066 (5.7 percent of the total) of these farms, those with annual sales of $1 million or more accounted for 75.2 percent of all vegetable sales in the country. On average, each of these very large vegetable farms sells about $2.1 million every year. Looking at this from the perspective of the small vegetable producer, the 50,575 farms with sales less than $1 million yearly sell on average only about $40,000 of produce each year. Not surprisingly, almost 40 percent of the million-dollar vegetable producers are found in California.[4] Other states with a substantial number of million-dollar producers include Washington ($n = 189$) and Oregon ($n = 188$) in the Pacific Northwest, Minnesota ($n = 113$) and Wisconsin ($n = 101$) in the Midwest, and Florida ($n = 210$), Georgia ($n = 125$), and North Carolina ($n = 125$) in the South. Together, these states account for two-thirds of the vegetables produced in the United States.

Fruit farms exhibit a similar degree of concentration, with 3.8 percent of all farms accounting for 58.6 percent of total sales. Even though there are fruit producers in virtually every state, a small handful of states dominate production. Of the 3,227 farms in the million-dollar-plus sales category, California with 1,909 (58.8 percent of the total) leads the list, followed by Florida with 347 farms (10.7 percent) and Washington with 324 farms (10.0 percent). Average sales on farms selling $1 million or more a year are approximately $2.3 million. On fruit farms with sales of less than $1 million yearly, average sales per farm are only $63,000 a year.

The corn, wheat, and soybean farm sectors still display considerably less concentration than other farm sectors. These farms form the backbone of agriculture in the American Midwest. Not only are there considerably more farms producing corn, wheat, and soybeans, compared with other commodities, but proportionately fewer of them have reached the $1 million sales mark. Further, the percentages of sales accounted for by those farms with $1 million or more in sales (i.e., 10.0 percent for corn, 11.4 percent for wheat, and 8.6 percent for soybeans) are well below those for other commodities.

But times may be rapidly changing for these farms as well. In 1996, the U.S. Congress passed the Freedom to Farm Act. This act was supposed to remove subsidies for grain farmers, ease regulations, and promote exports. In point of fact, it has led to a rapid restructuring of the farm sector.[5] Advanced biotechnologies are accelerating productivity. Farmers today are receiving near record low prices for basic commodities, due to overproduction. And the lack of alternative markets is forcing tens of thousands of Midwest farmers out of business. After the current shakeout runs its course, the farms that remain will be much larger in size, in terms of both acreage and volume of sales.

Changing Geography of Production

The changing geography of agricultural production is evident in tables 3.3 and 3.4. In 1910 eight of the top ten agricultural states were in the Midwest. Only New York, which produced fruits, vegetables, and dairy products for the booming East Coast cities, and Texas, which was a leading beef and vegetable

Table 3.3. Top Ten States Ranked by Agricultural Sales: 1910, 1950, 1997

Rank	1910	1950	1997
1	Iowa*	Texas*	California
2	Illinois*	California	Texas*
3	Texas*	Iowa*	Iowa*
4	Missouri	Illinois*	Nebraska*
5	Ohio	Minnesota*	Kansas*
6	Kansas*	Nebraska*	Illinois*
7	New York	Kansas*	Minnesota*
8	Indiana	Wisconsin	North Carolina
9	Nebraska*	Indiana	Florida
10	Minnesota*	Missouri	Wisconsin
	% of sales accounted by the top 10		
	48.7	50.8	52.8

Sources: Thirteenth Census of the United States, volumes 5–7 (Agriculture); U.S. Census of Agriculture, 1950; U.S. Census of Agriculture, 1997.

* States marked with asterisks (*) were ranked in the top 10 for each time period.

Table 3.4. Top Ten Counties Ranked by Agricultural Sales: 1950 and 1997

Rank	1950	1997	1997 sales ($1,000s)
1	Los Angeles, CA	Fresno, CA*	2,772,785
2	Fresno, CA*	Kern, CA*	1,968,513
3	Kern, CA*	Tulare, CA*	1,921,381
4	Tulare, CA*	Monterey, CA	1,749,747
5	Maricopa, AR	Weld, CO*	1,286,636
6	San Joaquin, CA*	Merced, CA	1,273,475
7	Weld, CO*	Stanislaus, CA*	1,208,524
8	Imperial, CA	San Joaquin, CA*	1,179,706
9	Lancaster, PA	Riverside, CA	1,047,525
10	Stanislaus, CA*	Yakima, WA	873,495

Sources: U.S. Census of Agriculture, 1950; U.S. Census of Agriculture, 1997.
Counties marked with asterisks (*) were ranked in the top 10 for each time period.

producer, fell outside of the Midwest. The development of an extensive ground transportation network over the next thirty years made the movement of fresh and processed fruits and vegetables both convenient and economical. By 1997, six of the top ten states were in the Midwest. These states produced most of the bulk commodities that fuel the agricultural economy. The other four states were in the South. And California, which was not a leading agricultural state in 1910, had jumped to the top of the list. Modern transportation, a near year-round growing season, and federally subsidized water combined to make California the nation's agricultural powerhouse. In 1997, California farms accounted for 11.7 percent of all agricultural sales in the United States.[6]

The importance of California's agriculture to the nation's food supply should not be underestimated. Eight of the ten leading agricultural counties in the United States, in terms of sales, are located in California. The largest of these counties, Fresno County, had over $2.7 billion in sales in 1997. There are twenty-two states in which gross agricultural sales are less than Fresno's $2.7 billion.

Distancing: Separating Production and Consumption

Brewster Kneen, a Canadian agricultural economist, uses the term "distancing" to indicate the process that separates people from the sources of their food and replaces diversified and sustainable food systems with a globalized, commodified system. According to Kneen, "Distancing most obviously means increasing the physical distance between the point at which food is actually grown or raised and the point at which it is consumed, as well as the extent to which the finished product is removed from its raw state by processing."[7] The processes of agricultural consolidation and concentration have resulted in a production system that is more often than not separated from where consumption occurs. Modern agricultural and food technologies have contributed to the distancing of food production from consumption in many ways. Plant breeders and other agricultural scientists have engineered stability and durability into commodities. Food processors take basic commodities and manufacture them into products that have very long shelf lives. And food scientists have developed preservation techniques to increase the time between when food is harvested or slaughtered and when it is consumed.[8]

Most states both import and export agricultural products. Complete agricultural or food self-sufficiency at the state level is probably not desirable, though a provocative paper by Michael Hamm, a nutritionist at Michigan State University, assesses the potential for a localized food supply in New Jersey. As Hamm notes, "If sustainable in the long term implies greater local food production within an ecosystem/community context then we need to see if the potential exists within some area to produce adequate supplies of food."[9] Although New Jersey is the most densely population state in the nation, he points out that there are still approximately 600,000 acres of cropland and 160,000 acres of pasture in the state. Drawing on a broad range of data sources and using a nutritional analysis framework, Hamm concludes that if certain conditions are met, the potential exists for producing all the food needed for the population of New Jersey within its borders.

If a densely populated state like New Jersey has the potential, theoretically at least, to feed all its residents, the prospects for other states to feed their residents must be at least as favorable. In other words, there is probably an untapped potential to relocalize large segments of local food economies.

Control of Farmland

The effects of the industrialization and globalization of agriculture can also be seen in patterns of farmland ownership and control. A global system of food production, one that is increasingly coming under the control of large national and multinational corporations, has begun to refashion how and, more importantly, where food is produced. Driving the global/industrial system of farming is the continual search by agribusiness firms for areas of low-cost production. In a global system of food production, labor and capital flow to places where maximum profits can be extracted. In this system, farmland becomes a "staging area" for the production of food, and given that the supply of farmland exceeds demand, there is little incentive to protect any particular tracts of land from nonagricultural development.[10]

Land, unlike the other factors of production, is not geographically mobile. However, as capital and labor migrate from place to place, land has the potential to be brought into and taken out of production from one growing season to the next, depending on where maximum profits can be extracted at any given time.

In most nonextractive enterprises, land serves as a "condition" of production in the sense that it provides the space or location for an economic activity (e.g., the land on which a manufacturing plant is situated). For most agricultural activities, however, land is a "means" of production. As the British geographer Richard Munton notes: "For most systems of farming the soil itself provides the growth medium, while acting as a store for capital inputs of varying duration, ranging from the ephemeral (chemical nutrients) to the long term (irrigation systems). As land varies in its fertility and in its relative location, these characteristics confer advantages on some parcels of land at the expense of others."[11]

Over the long term, technological advances in the agricultural sciences will continue to raise productivity levels on most farmland around the world. Whether production increases can match growth rates attained over the past forty to fifty years remains an open question at this point. However, over the short term we are likely to see more and more farmland move out of the hands of the people who work it. Absentee landlords are becoming a permanent fixture on the American agricultural landscape.

A global system of agricultural production operates at its highest economic efficiency when the factors of production can be freely substituted for one another. If land can be brought into and taken out of production on a seasonal basis, then it acquires the same degree fluidity as capital, labor, and management. In California, which produces the largest agricultural sales of any state in the nation, for example, the amount of farmland on which the same individual (or set of individuals) was both owner and operator decreased by almost 10 million acres between 1950 and 1997. However, the amount of farmland that was owned by someone other than the operator and leased to the operator by a neighboring farmer or absentee landlord increased by over 1 million acres during this time period. Today almost half of all the land that is in agricultural production in California is absentee-owned.

Similarly, in Texas, the second-largest agricultural sales producer in the nation, the amount of farmland that is owned and operated by the same individual or set of individuals decreased by 21 million acres since 1950, while the amount of rented land increased by almost 7 million acres. Today, over half of the farmland in Delaware, Illinois, Indiana, Iowa, Kansas, Louisiana, and North Dakota is owned by someone other than the person who farms it.

It is difficult to empirically evaluate the social and economic consequences of the shift to absentee ownership of large tracts of farmland. Land, which once anchored labor, capital, and management to a particular place and formed the foundation of a family-based system of farming, is increasingly being put into a "reserve pool" from which it can be brought into or taken out of production as global market forces dictate. Control of the food system, then, is shifting from local production and regional and national processing to large-scale, global firms.

Labor Intensification

Until quite recently, agricultural development in the United States has been characterized by abundant land, a steady stream of labor-saving and land-extending technologies, and a relatively scarce pool of labor. The "family farm" mode of economic organization incorporated all members of the household into meeting the labor needs of the farm. When the amount of work became too great for the existing family labor pool, one or two hired hands were added to the farm. However, unlike many nonagricultural enterprises, especially manufacturing, the ability to "efficiently" integrate a large hired labor force into most farm enterprises was constrained by the unique aspects of agriculture. The disjuncture between "labor time" and "production time," noted by the sociologists Susan Mann and James Dickinson and others, worked against the development of a labor-intensive system of industrial agriculture.[12] Don Albrecht and Steve Murdock, rural sociologists at Texas A&M University, note in this regard, "farm production consists of stages that are typically separated by waiting periods because the biological processes involved take time to complete. [And] . . . unlike production in other industries where commodities are produced continuously throughout the year, crop production is seasonal."[13]

Given the difficulty of adapting agriculture to accommodate an industrial-like labor force, one might expect that the amount of hired labor on American farms would remain constant or more likely decline. And, in fact, during most the twentieth century the number of hired workers on American farms slowly, but steadily, went down. However, beginning in the late 1970s and early 1980s, as the first waves of industrialization swept over the agricultural landscape, the number of nonfamily hired laborers began to increase.

Counting farmworkers is a tricky business. Much agricultural work is seasonal. Legal and illegal workers float into and out of the labor force. And government agencies that are responsible for keeping track of the nation's farmworkers do not often agree on basic definitions.[14] However, the Census of Agriculture has provided a window that allows for a relatively straightforward comparison of the number of workers per farm in 1950 and 1997. In what is no doubt an administrative fluke, in both of these agricultural census years, data were collected using a similar set of questions. Thus, looking at these data we know that there were 1,555,269 nonfamily workers employed on all American farms in 1950. By 1997, there were 3,352,028. It should be remembered that during this same period the number of farms in the United States decreased by over 3 million.

California, a state whose farmers have led the way down the industrial agriculture path, reported hiring 163,000 farmworkers in 1950. This figure includes full-time, part-time, and migrant workers. By 1997, California farmers were employing almost 550,000 farmworkers. Florida saw the number of hired workers on its farms increase from 67,000 in 1950 to 125,000 in 1997. The additional farmworkers were added during a time that Florida lost over 35 percent of its farmland and nearly 40 percent of its farmers. And North Carolina saw the number of hired workers more than double, from 54,000 in 1950 to 127,000 in 1997. This influx of hired labor occurred at the same time that North Carolina was losing over half of its farmland and over 80 percent of its farmers. In all these cases, the growth of the hired workforce on farms coupled with the decrease in the number of farms and the loss of farmland signaled a change from traditional family farming to industrial-like agricultural production.

In most states it was not the typical family-labor farm that was adding a hired man (or woman) or two to extend its operation and capture some additional economies of scale. Instead, it was a new breed of labor-intensive, industrial-like operators that accounted for the dramatic increase in hired workers. The numbers of farms that employed ten or more hired workers went up everywhere and especially in those states where the industrial model of farming was taking a firm hold. In California there has been a threefold increase in these labor-intensive farms in the past fifty years. Today over 9,500 California farms, each employing on average almost fifty workers, account for almost 85 percent of all hired farm labor in the state. In Florida these labor-intensive farms also average over fifty workers and account for nearly 80 percent of all hired farm labor in the state.

Supply Chains

The contours of the industrial model of agricultural and food production have come into bold relief in the last decades. The pieces fell into place as land, labor, and capital were brought together in a deliberate and coordinated fashion and orchestrated by a small handful of very large and very powerful agribusiness firms. To ensure large quantities of standardized and uniform products, food processors entered into formal contracts with individual farmers. Although there are no systematic data available on contract production, Rick Welsh notes that "since 1960, contracts and vertically integrated operations have accounted for an ever-larger share of total U.S. agricultural production."[15] Today, in the United States, about 85 percent of processed vegetables are grown under contract and 15 percent are produced on large corporate farms. Contract farming allows food processors to exert significant control over their agricultural suppliers. While the processor benefits from these arrangements, the major disadvantage to the farmer is a loss of independence. Many contracts specify quantity, quality, price, and delivery date, and in some instances the processor is completely involved in the management of the farm, including input provision.

Contract farming has also increased farm size. Economies of scale dictate that processors are more inclined to work with large farmers whenever possible. It has been suggested that the processor's ability to award or refuse a contract has contributed to differences in profitability between large and small producers and accelerated the process of farm concentration.[16] According to Mark Drabenstott, an economist at the Kansas City Federal Reserve Bank, a more tightly choreographed food system is emerging throughout the country. "The key component in this choreography is a business alliance known as a supply chain. In a supply chain, farmers sign a contract with a major food company to deliver precisely grown farm products on a pre-set schedule."[17]

The spread of contract farming is resulting in a reconfiguration of production at the local level, because it is the processor and not the farmer who determines what commodity is produced and where. This requirement imposes a distance limit on producers and leads to narrowly defined supply areas revolving around the location of the processing plants. In the process of this transformation, the ties between farmers and processors have been restructured.

For farmers in the United States and elsewhere, the globalization of the food system means that a much smaller number of producers will articulate with a small number of processors in a highly integrated business alliance. Drabenstott estimates that "40 or fewer chains will control nearly all U.S. pork production in a matter of a few years, and that these chains will engage a *mere fraction* [italics added] of the 100,000 hog farms now scattered across the nation."[18] In a similar vein, the CEO of Dairy Farms of America (the largest U.S. dairy cooperative), Gary Hanman, recently noted, "We would need only 7,468 farms [out of over 100,000 today] with 1,000 cows if they produced 20,857 pounds of milk which is the average of the top four milk producing states."[19] The consequences are clear: ". . . supply chains will locate in relatively few rural communities. And with fewer farmers and fewer suppliers where they do locate, the economic impact will be different from the commodity agriculture of the past."[20]

CHAPTER 4

The Global Supply Chain

The Global Food System

The contours of a truly global system of agriculture and food production are quickly coming into focus. From the biotechnology laboratories to the dinner table, large multinational corporations are taking control of where, when, and how food is produced, processed, and distributed. As Bill Heffernan, a rural sociologist at the University of Missouri, recently noted in a 1999 report to the National Farmers Union, "The major concern about concentration of the food system focuses on the control exercised by a handful of firms over decision-making throughout the food system. The question is who is able to make decisions about buying and selling products in a marketplace."[1]

Heffernan identifies a handful of "food-chain clusters" that are taking control of the food system from the "gene to the supermarket shelf." These include (1) Cargill/Monsanto (2) Conagra, and (3) Novartis/ADM.[2] In a similar vein, the Rural Advancement Foundation International (RAFI) published "The Gene Giants: Masters of the Universe," which describes how transnational firms are coming to dominate the market for agrochemicals, seeds, pharmaceuticals, and animal feed and products. According to RAFI, the food and beverage giants are the "true titans" of the "life industry." Total retail sales of food worldwide are estimated at $2 trillion.[3] As genetic engineering and related technologies become more widely used in agricultural production and food processing, transnational firms in the food and beverage industry are likely to form alliances with the seed, biotechnology, and agrochemical companies that Heffernan discusses.

Today, mass-production food processors and distributors along with mass-market retailers have become dominant fixtures in the American food economy. These large-scale producers and retailers provide abundant quantities of relatively inexpensive, standardized goods. The degree of concentration has reached the point where the ten largest multinational food processors control over 60 percent of the food and beverages sold in the United States. According to *Prepared Foods,* the leading trade publication for the food and beverage industry, the list of the largest food processing companies is led by Swiss giant Nestlé (see table 4.1). Nestlé had sales of over $46 billion in 2001. Kraft Foods, which was recently spun off from Philip Morris, is the largest U.S.-based food company, with sales of over $38 billion. Overall, seven of the ten largest food processors are headquartered in the United States.

The sheer size of the multinational food giants has important consequences for farmers and their farms, not only in the United States, but around the world as well. According to the geographer Philip Hart, "Size brings economic power and this is particularly significant when set against the structure of the farming industry with its large number of relatively small producers. Some of the most dramatic recent changes in agricultural marketing reflect the power of these new markets to extract their requirements from the farming industry."[4] Large food processors and retailers centralize their purchases of farm products. Because they seek mass

Table 4.1. Ten Largest Food-Processing Corporations: 2001

Company	Headquarters	Sales ($ million)
Nestlé	Switzerland	46,628
Kraft Foods	USA	38,119
ConAgra	USA	27,630
PepsiCo	USA	26,935
Unilever	UK	26,672
Archer, Daniels, Midland	USA	23,454
Cargill	USA	21,500
Coca Cola	USA	20,092
Diageo*	UK	16,644
Mars	USA	15,300

Source: *Prepared Foods,* December 2002, p. 83.
* Diageo sold off its Pillsbury Division to General Mills in late 2001.

quantities of standardized and uniform products, they have considerable power in dictating how and where agricultural production takes place.

During the 1970s and 1980s a rather dramatic transformation began to take place in the processing side of the food industry. A wave of mergers and acquisitions transformed what was at the time a system of large, nationally oriented food companies into a global system of multinational food giants. In the process of this transformation, the ties between farmers and processors were restructured. The story of Green Giant is revealing.

The Jolly Green Giant as a Corporate Migrant

The Green Giant company began life as the Minnesota Valley Canning Company in Le Sueur, Minnesota, in 1903. The company grew steadily through the 1940s and in 1950 changed its name to Green Giant. Although the canned and frozen vegetable business stagnated in the 1950s, the 1960s saw a return to profitability for the company. During the 1960s and 1970s, Green Giant expanded its operations beyond simply processing vegetables. It opened a chain of restaurants and sandwich shops along with a number of Green Giant Home and Garden Centers. While these ventures were of dubious financial success, the company remained profitable throughout the 1970s.[5]

In 1979, Pillsbury acquired the Green Giant company in what appeared to be a friendly takeover. Although at the time of the takeover Green Giant had expanded its operations beyond canning and packaging vegetables to include restaurants, meat products, and fruits, after the takeover Pillsbury divested itself of everything except the vegetable business. In turn, Pillsbury streamlined Green Giant's vegetable business and turned it into a very profitable venture.

In 1989, Pillsbury, which was an emerging food conglomerate in and of itself, was acquired by Grand Metropolitan, a UK-based multinational food giant. Grand Metropolitan's plans for Green Giant were to make it "the number one vegetable company in the *world* by the year 2000."[6]

To accomplish this daunting feat, Grand Met divested Green Giant of all of its production and processing facilities. Green Giant closed many of its processing plants. Those that were not closed were sold either to Seneca Foods, J. R. Simplot (a Boise, Idaho, packer), or to United Refrigerated Cold Storage in Atlanta. These divestitures were made to "increase competitiveness and customer service." According to Ian Martin, the CEO of Grand Metropolitan, the goal was to make Green Giant "a true international brand with its cartoon figure [the Jolly Green Giant] in line with all of the green values of ecology."[7]

In the 1990s, then, Green Giant became the first "virtual" food corporation. Today it owns no production or processing facilities. Green Giant procures the vegetables it needs by entering into contracts with farmers around the world. It then outsources the canning and packaging of these commodities to companies like Seneca Foods, which operates twenty-two packing plants in seven states. As Seneca Foods proudly proclaims, "Give us your recipe and your specifications and we'll provide a finished product that you'll be proud to put your label on."[8]

In late 1997 Grand Metropolitan merged with Guinness Ltd. of Ireland to form an even larger multinational food giant, Diageo. In 1997, Diageo sold almost $19 billion in food and beverage products. It had become the eighth-largest food and beverage company in the world.

And the Green Giant story continues to turn. In 2001, Diageo sold its Pillsbury Division to General Mills for $10.4 billion. The Pillsbury Doughboy and the Jolly Green Giant came home to Minnesota, but only as brand names. As part of the deal, Diageo received 134 million shares of General Mills, valued at $ 5.9 billion. When the deal closed, Diageo owned a 32 percent stake in General Mills. While the stories are a bit different for each, most of the first-generation canners and packers have been swallowed up to become part of the large multinational corporations that are rapidly taking control of the food system. In some instances, such as Green Giant, it is only the brand name that is being sold, since the productive assets of the company such as farms and factories were sold off years ago.

Grocery Wars

Since 1990, the retail sector of the food industry has seen the emergence of five major players: Kroger, Wal-Mart, Albertson's, Safeway, and Ahold USA. In the early 1990s, these five retailers accounted for only about 20 percent of retail sales. Together, these five firms now account for over 40 percent of food retail sales (see table 4.2). However, as Phil Kaufman, an agricultural economist at USDA notes, ". . . the effect of consolidation on consumers is related primarily to increases in local market concentration—the combined sales of the largest firms expressed as a share of the total local market sales."[9] Average market concentration of the top four retailers in individual metropolitan areas stands at about 75 percent. And there are several metropolitan areas in which the top four firms account for 90 percent or more of sales.[10]

Almost all of the large food retailers cite lower costs and greater efficiencies as the primary benefits of consolidation. As size increases, procurement, marketing, and distribution costs presumably decrease. Further, to lower their operating costs, the large food retailers are centralizing management and control at their headquarters. Finally, by forming supply chains with global processors, the large retailers are able to streamline procurement and distribution of products.

Table 4.2. Ten Largest Grocery Store Chains in the United States: 2001

Company	Number of stores	Sales ($ million)
Kroger	3,211	50,700
Albertson's	2,573	38,300
Safeway	1,762	34,301
Ahold USA	1,446	23,200
Wal-Mart Supercenters*	1,060	20,100
Sam's Club	498	18,396
Costco Wholesale Group	363	17,690
Delhaize America	1,466	15,200
Publix Super Markets	675	14,742
Winn-Dixie Stores	1,150	12,903

Source: Food Marketing Institute: *http://www.fmi.org/facts_figs/faq/top_retailers.htm*
* Wal-Mart Supercenters sales are for groceries only.

Corporate Reach: The Men and Women behind the Food System

The large agribusiness firms are run by seemingly faceless boards of directors. A recent study of the food-processing industry showed that only 138 men and women sit on the boards of directors of the ten firms that account for over half of all the food sold in America.[11]

The boards of directors of most large U.S. corporations are composed of individuals who share a great deal in common. Two well-known sociologists, C. Wright Mills and William Domhoff have examined the characteristics and behaviors of America's economic elite.[12] They found that individuals who are recruited to sit on the boards of large American corporations come from similar social and economic backgrounds and belong to the same social circles. They interact with one another through memberships in the same clubs, churches, and organizations.

A board of directors is the ultimate source of power and control in a corporation. Corporate directors are responsible only to stockholders. It is the directors' job to protect the stockholders' interests and to monitor corporate management's policies. According to the British sociologist Stephen Hill, not only does the board of directors monitor the state of the company, its members also engage in strategic planning. More particularly, the job of directors is "to appoint appropriate managers to the various businesses and to ensure there is appropriate succession planning . . . and . . . to make specific decisions in relation to matters of particular importance such as capital expenditures above certain limits, acquisitions, disinvestment decisions, capital increases."[13]

It is boards of directors that make decisions to "expand, close, or move factories and offices."[14] For example, Grand

Metropolitan's decision to sell off or close all its Green Giant processing plants in the early 1990s and disrupt the lives of thousands of workers, their families, and their communities was made by a handful of men and women, most of whom were not residents of the United States. More recently, the multinational chicken and pork producer Tyson Foods announced that it would close its pork-processing plant in North Carolina and lay off five hundred workers in an effort to increase profitability, while Frito-Lay, a subsidiary of Pepsico, announced plans to close plants in North Carolina, Georgia, Mississippi, and Massachusetts and let go almost nine hundred workers.[15] On the chessboard of the global food system, factories are pieces that are sacrificed or moved in the quest for profits. The fate of the workers and communities left behind is seldom a topic of concern in the corporate boardroom.[16]

In the food and beverage sector, the boards of directors play a major role in shaping the food *choices* of American consumers. The proliferation of fatty snack foods, sugared cereals, highly processed "convenience foods" (e.g., frozen, canned, or packaged dinners), caffeinated beverages, and the like have been directly linked to nutrition-related health problems such as obesity, high blood pressure, high blood cholesterol, and diabetes.[17] These types of foods are sources of tremendous profits for the large multinational food giants.

A representative excerpt from the 2003 *Annual Report* of the Pepsico Corporation gives a good indication of what consumers, both here and abroad, are likely to find on their supermarket shelves. Under the heading of "Brands and Goodwill" we read:

> We sell products under a number of brand names around the world, many of which were developed by us. . . . We also purchase brands and goodwill in acquisitions. . . . We believe that

a brand has an indefinite life if it has significant market share in a stable macroeconomic environment, and a history of strong revenue and cash flow performance that we expect to continue for the foreseeable future. If these perpetual brand criteria are not met, brands are amortized over their expected useful lives, which generally range from five to twenty years. Determining the expected life of a brand requires considerable management judgment and is based on an evaluation of a number of factors, including the competitive environment, market share, brand history and the macroeconomic environment of the country in which the brand is sold.[18]

As with most oligopolistic industries, the food and beverage industry generally speaks with one voice when it comes to labor, trade, environmental, and food safety issues.[19] Of course, there is remarkable overlap in the nature and range of products produced and distributed by the global food and beverage corporations (e.g., Coke vs. Pepsi, Lays Potato Chips vs. Pringles, Lean Cuisine vs. Healthy Choice). This is not surprising, since the large multinational corporations can be viewed as a confederation of firms that share similar product lines and marketing strategies. Because the men and women who sit on the boards of directors come from a similar background and share similar work histories, they are likely to share a common worldview when it comes to managing these globally oriented food firms. The ultimate result is that these few individuals decide food choices for most American consumers.

A food system dominated by a handful of large corporations and governed by a small set of like-minded individuals offers consumers little real "choice." Innovation in these firms is linked to devising better *marketing* strategies for a narrow range of "basic" products (i.e., soft drinks, breakfast cereals, snack and convenience foods, and the like). The fact that over twelve thousand new products are introduced each year (most of which fail) suggests that the food industry is not responding to consumer demand but is rather blindly offering consumers sets of repackaged, reformulated, and reengineered products in hopes that a few of them will turn out to boost corporate profits.

Whither the Poor Consumer?

What does all this mean for the consumer? The consolidation of the food industry clearly means less competition and lower costs for the producer. But recent research suggests that the consumer may not benefit. A study by a group of agricultural economists at the University of Nebraska-Lincoln and the University of Connecticut shows that concentration in the food-processing industry has resulted in higher consumer prices in most sectors due in part to the ability of oligopolies to set prices.[20]

A consolidated, corporately controlled food and agriculture system is able to provide vast quantities of standardized fare. The foundation of this system rests on a set of very large farms articulating with a small number of global food processors, who in turn link with another small number of very large and increasingly global food retailers. For the system to run *efficiently* it must standardize and rationalize both production and transaction costs all along the food chain. The smaller the number of players in the system, the easier it is to standardize and rationalize.

Production costs are lowered by adopting mass-production techniques to grow crops, raise livestock, and process and package these commodities. For the industrial type of agriculture to continue to expand, it must convert family farms into factory farms. The transformation of family farms into factory farms requires not only a change in the size of the farm operation but a change in management strategies as well. It means locking the farmer into the orbit of the large agribusiness corporation.

Stewart Smith, an agricultural economist from Maine, examined the distribution of economic activity within the agricultural sector of the economy. He found that in 1910 farming accounted for 41 percent of the industry's economic activity. By 1990, this had fallen to 9 percent. On the other hand, the input sector saw its share of activity grow from 15 percent in 1910 to 24 percent in 1990, while the marketing sector went from 44 percent to 67 percent during this period.[21] The data in table 4.3 indicate that this represents a shift of billions of dollars from farmers to agribusiness. Indeed, farmers receive less in real dollars today than they did in 1910, while the dollar amount taken by marketers has increased over sixfold. As Eric Schlosser notes in *Fast Food Nation,* "Farmers and cattle ranchers are losing their independence, essentially becoming hired hands for the agribusiness giants. . . . Family farms are now being replaced by gigantic corporate farms with absentee owners."[22]

Factory farming is making inroads among many commodities. Large dry-lot dairies account for the bulk of milk

Table 4.3. Share of Economic Activity within the Agricultural Sector Accounted for by Farmers, Input Suppliers, and Marketers: 1910 and 1990

Year	Farmer	Input supplier	Marketer
1910	41% $24 billion	15% $13 billion	44% $35 billion
1990	9% $23 billion	24% $58 billion	67% $216 billion

production in many states. Confinement hog operations are crowding out family hog farms in the Midwest. And beef production has moved to huge industrial feedlots in Colorado and other western states.[23] Already we see an almost total conversion to factory farming among poultry farmers. The Web site www.factoryfarming.com has excellent descriptions of factory-farming techniques for eggs, pork, dairy, beef, poultry, and fish. Here is a brief excerpt for poultry.

Nearly ten billion chickens . . . are being hatched in the U.S. every year. These birds are typically crowded by the thousand into huge factory-like warehouses where they can barely move. Chickens are given less than half a square foot of space per bird. . . . Today's meat chickens have been genetically altered to grow twice as fast, and twice as large as their ancestors. . . . An industry journal explains "broilers [chickens] now grow so rapidly that the heart and lungs are not developed well enough to support the remainder of the body, resulting in congestive heart failure and tremendous death losses." . . . Chickens . . . are taken to the slaughterhouse in crates stacked on the back of trucks. The birds are either pulled from the crates, or the crates are lifted off the truck, often with a crane or forklift, and then the birds are dumped onto a conveyor belt. As the birds are unloaded, some fall onto the ground instead of landing on the assembly line conveyor belt. Slaughterhouse workers intent upon "processing" thousands of birds every hour, don't have the time nor the inclination to pick up individuals who fall through the cracks. . . . Once inside the slaughterhouse, fully conscious birds are hung by their feet from metal shackles on a moving rail. The first station on most poultry slaughterhouse assembly lines is the stunning tank, where the birds' heads are submerged in an electrified bath of water. . . . After passing through the stunning tank, the birds' throats are slashed, usually by a mechanical blade, and blood begins rushing out of their bodies. Inevitably, the blade misses some birds who then proceed to the next station on the assembly line, the scalding tank. Here they are submerged in boiling hot water. Birds missed by the killing blade are boiled alive. This occurs so commonly, affecting millions of birds every year. . . . [24]

For farmers in the United States and elsewhere, the globalization of production means that the markets for their products have become very unstable. Unless a farmer is able to enter into a long-term contract with a canner, packer, or other purchaser, his/her ability to make long-term plans is seriously compromised.

As Bill Heffernan notes, "The centralized food system that continues to emerge was never voted on by the people of this country, or for that matter, the people of the world. It is the product of deliberate decisions made by a very few powerful human actors."[25] A small set of individuals control an empire that accounts for most of the products we see on supermarket shelves. The social, economic, and political costs of a corporately managed and controlled agriculture and food system are seldom tallied. In the United States today, food has become simply a commodity that generates profits for large corporations.

CHAPTER 5

Toward a Civic Agriculture

Moving toward Civic Agriculture

Agriculture and food production is being restructured in the United States. On the one hand, large-scale, well-managed, capital-intensive, technologically sophisticated, industrial-like operations are becoming tightly tied into a network of national and global food producers. These farms will be producing large quantities of highly standardized bulk commodities that will feed into large national and multinational integrators and processors. A few hundred very large farms will account for most of the gross agricultural sales.

However, a substantial number of smaller-scale, locally oriented, flexibly organized farms and food producers are taking root throughout the United States. These are part and parcel of what I call the new *civic agriculture*.[1] And if the current trends continue, civic agriculture will likely expand in scope to become an enduring feature of the agricultural landscape. These farms and food processors will fill the geographic and economic spaces that have been passed over or ignored by large-scale, industrial producers. Civic agricultural farms and food processors will articulate with consumer demand for locally produced and processed food.

Civic agriculture is the embedding of local agricultural and food production in the community. Civic agriculture is not only a source of family income for the farmer and food processor; civic agricultural enterprises contribute to the health and vitality of communities in a variety of social, economic, political, and cultural ways.[2] For example, civic agriculture increases agricultural literacy by directly linking consumers to producers. Likewise, civic agricultural enterprises have a much higher local economic multiplier than farms or processors that are producing for the global mass market. Dollars spent for locally produced food and agricultural products circulate several times more through the local community than money spent for products manufactured by multinational corporations and sold in national supermarket chains.

Civic agriculture should not be confused with civic farmers. Farmers who vote in local elections, who sit on school boards, who are active members of local service clubs such as Rotary, Lions, or Kiwanis, and who otherwise participate in the civic affairs of their communities may be seen as "good citizens." However, a farm or food operation that is not integrated into the economic structure of the local community, that produces for the export market, that relies on nonlocal hired labor, and that provides few benefits for its workers is not a civic enterprise, regardless of the civic engagement of its operator.

Obviously, no agricultural or food enterprise is without some civic merit. However, large-scale, contract poultry and hog operations—farmers who sell only to large food corporations such as Tyson's, Perdue, or Hormel—would lie at the far outside end of civicness. Likewise, large-scale, absentee-owned, factory-like fruit and vegetable farms that rely on large numbers of migrant workers and sell their produce for export around the world would not be deemed very civic.

Smaller-scale agriculture and food ventures that are tied to the community through direct marketing or integration into local circuits of food processing and procurement would embody the civic concept.[3] Taken together, the enterprises that make up and support civic agriculture can been seen as part of a community's *problem-solving capacity*. The locally based organizational, associational, and institutional component of the agriculture and food system is at the heart of civic agriculture. Local producer and marketing cooperatives, regional trade associations, and community-based farm and food organizations are part of the underlying structure that supports civic agriculture.

The conventional approach to production agriculture has been to treat the farm operator as a manager and as an individual "problem solver." The role of USDA's Cooperative Extension Service, which is still the primary educational outreach organization for farmers, has been to provide each producer with the knowledge, skills, and information necessary to make the best decisions within the parameters of his or her own farm. The individual, not the community, has been the sole locus of attention (for program development) and of action (for outreach efforts). Farmers who "failed" to make a profit and subsequently went out of business, whether or not they had followed the prescriptions of Cooperative Extension, were deemed "bad managers."[4]

Civic agriculture, by contrast, is a locally organized system of agriculture and food production characterized by networks of producers who are bound together by place. Civic agriculture embodies a commitment to developing and strengthening an economically, environmentally, and socially sustainable system of agriculture and food production that relies on local resources and serves local markets and consumers. The imperative to earn a profit is filtered through a set of cooperative and mutually supporting social relations. Community problem solving rather than individual competition is the foundation of civic agriculture.[5]

Theoretical Underpinnings of Civic Agriculture

The theoretical and conceptual underpinnings of a more localized agriculture and food system were set forth over fifty years ago in two studies published by the U.S. government as part of a congressional inquiry into the role of small business in the American economy. Coming out of World War II, big business had become the primary engine for military production. The consequences for workers and communities of an economy organized around large-scale economic enterprises were unknown. At least some members of Congress felt compelled to hold hearings on this subject. As part of the hearings, two empirical studies were commissioned to examine the relationship between the concentration of economic power at the community level and the social and economic well-being of local residents. The thesis advanced in both of these studies was that communities in which the economic base was composed of a plethora of relatively small, locally owned firms would manifest higher levels of social, economic, and political welfare and well-being than communities where the economic base was dominated by a few large, absentee-owned firms.

The first report, by the sociologist C. Wright Mills and his colleague Melville Ulmer, *Small Business and Civic Welfare,* focused on manufacturing-dependent communities.[6] Mills and Ulmer were interested in understanding the "effects of big and small business on city life." Using three matched pairs of American cities in New York, New Hampshire, and Michigan,[7] Mills and Ulmer showed that communities in which the economic base was composed of many small, locally owned firms manifested higher levels of well-being than communities where the economic base was dominated by large, absentee-owned firms. In particular, they found that the small-business communities provided their residents with a considerably more balanced economic life than did the big-business communities. They also reported that the general level of economic opportunity was considerably higher in the small-business communities. They attributed the differences in well-being and opportunity to differences in industrial organization—that is, specifically to the dominance of big business on the one hand and the prevalence of small business on the other. In the forward to their congressional report, Senator James E. Murray, chairman of the special committee that had commissioned the study, noted that ". . . for the first time objective scientific data show that communities in which small businesses predominate have a higher level of civic welfare than comparable communities dominated by big business."[8]

To explain differences they had found in social and economic well being, Mills and Ulmer turned to two interevening variables. First, they contended that the level of civic engagement in a community was directly related to levels of socio-economic welfare. According to Mills and Ulmer, "Civic spirit may be said to exist in a city where there is widespread participation in civic affairs on the part of those able to benefit a community by voluntary management of civic enterprises. These enterprises may consist of attempts to improve the parks, obtain better schools, make the streets broader, etc."[9] Simply put, communities with high levels of civic spirit manifested higher levels of well-being and welfare.

Second, and more importantly, Mills and Ulmer identified the *economically independent middle class* as the driving force behind civic engagement. Not only was the economically independent middle class more prevalent in communities not dominated by big business, but it was this group of economic actors that "usually took the lead in voluntary management of civic enterprises."[10]

Mills and Ulmer offered several reasons why the economically independent middle class has "traditionally been the chief participant in the management of civic enterprises. For one thing, he [*sic*] usually has some time and money available with which to interest himself in these matters. He is, on average, fairly well educated. His work in conducting a small business trains him for initiative and responsibility. He is thrown into constant contact with the administrative and political figures of the city. . . . Furthermore, the small businessman often stands to benefit personally as a result of civic improvement. . . . "[11]

Walter Goldschmidt's Landmark Study

In the second empirical study commissioned by the U.S. Senate, *Small Business and the Community,* the anthropologist Walter Goldschmidt contrasted "communities of large and small farms" in the Central Valley of California.[12] Arvin, the large farm community, is located in Kern County, south of Bakersfield. It was dominated by farms that were considerably bigger than those found in Dinuba, the smaller-farm community. Dinuba is located north of Arvin in Tulare County, near Fresno. According to Goldschmidt, ". . . the differences between average farm size are great—in the neighborhood of 9 to 1 when taken on an acreage basis, 5 to

1 in value of products, and 3 to 1 if adjusted for intensity of operations. Nine-tenths of all farm land is operated in units of 160 acres of more in Arvin as against one-fourth in Dinuba." However, both Arvin and Dinuba were similar in population size, shared value systems, and social customs and were "part of a common system of agricultural production, best understood as industrialized."[13]

Goldschmidt sought to relate "the scale of farm operations" to a set of "social and economic factors [that would reflect] the qualities of society in the two communities."[14] He found that residents in the community dominated by large-scale, corporately controlled farming had a lower standard of living and quality of life than residents in the community where production was dispersed among a large number of smaller farms. In particular he found:

1. Arvin had more wage laborers than Dinuba, while Dinuba had more entrepreneurs.
2. Arvin had lower living conditions.
3. Arvin had a more unstable population.
4. Arvin had a poorer physical appearance.
5. Social services were poorer in Arvin.
6. Poorer schools, parks, and youth services were found in Arvin.
7. Arvin had a dearth of social services.
8. Dinuba had more religious institutions.
9. There was a higher degree of community loyalty in Dinuba.
10. In Arvin, fewer community decisions were made by community residents.
11. Arvin displayed greater social segregation.
12. Dinuba had more retail trade.

Based on these observations, Goldschmidt concluded the following: "The scale of operations that developed in Arvin inevitably had one clear and direct effect on the community: It skewed the occupation structure so that the majority of the population could only subsist by working as wage labor for others. . . . The occupation structure of the community, with a great majority of wage workers . . . has had a series of direct effects upon social conditions in the community."[15] In other words, differences in social and economic welfare between the large-farm and the small-farm communities were directly the result of worker exploitation.

Unlike Mills and Ulmer, Goldschmidt did not integrate the civically engaged independent middle class into his explanatory framework. However, he did acknowledge the presence of this group in his study. For example, he noted that "the small farm community is a population of middle class persons with a high degree of stability in income and tenure, and a strong economic and social interest in their community."[16] Elsewhere, Goldschmidt articulated the relationship between civic engagement and the independent middle class. According to Goldschmidt, "civic leadership in Dinuba . . . rests largely with a small group of merchants, teachers, and other professional persons."[17] And he went on to elaborate the rich organizational and associational life in the small farm community.

Production Districts

The perspective set forth by C. Wright Mills and Melville Ulmer and by Walter Goldschmidt in the 1940s fits within a renewed interest in industrial/production districts that are organized around smaller-scale enterprises, including family farms.[18] Jonathon Zeitlin, a professor of history, sociology, and industrial relations at the University of Wisconsin, has noted that smaller-scale, locally oriented production and distribution systems "require a broad set of infrastructural institutions and services to coordinate relationships among economic actors" and to compensate for the inefficiencies of a fragmented system of food production.[19] Relatedly, Charles Sabel, a political scientist at Columbia University, notes that the success and survival of locally based economic systems is directly tied to the collective efforts of the community to which they belong.[20] Similarly, the sociologist Charles Perrow states that "small organizations are linked together by a sense of community of fate, rather than a link based on employees sharing the goals of the owners and top executives of a big organization."[21]

The emergence of production districts as an organizing frame for modern, technologically sophisticated economies is being complemented by a body of scholarship and writing on civil society, civic community, and civic engagement. Social scientists, especially political scientists and sociologists who have adopted a "civic" perspective, are now challenging the assumption that a more globally integrated and corporately managed economy is the "best" and perhaps "only" development path that will lead to enhanced social and economic welfare for workers and communities.[22] The civil society perspective meshes with the belief that small- to medium-size production enterprises can serve as the foundation of modern industrial economies. At the local level, the civic community is one in which residents are bound to a place by a plethora of local institutions and organizations.[23] Business enterprises are embedded in institutional and organizational networks.[24] And the community, not the corporation, is the source of personal identity, the topic of social discourse, and the foundation for social cohesion.[25]

Two Models of Agricultural Development

While a comprehensive theory of civic community as it relates to agricultural development is still being constructed, the outlines of such a theory can be discerned. In table 5.1, I compare selected dimensions of the dominant commodity-focused and market-based approach to agricultural development with an approach based on civic community. There are

Table 5.1. Two Models of Agricultural Development

Conventional agriculture	Civic agriculture
Social Theory	

Neoclassical economics:
    Modernization
    Globalization
	Pragmatism:
	    Sustainability
	    Civic community

Biological Theory	

Experimental biology:
    Reductionist
    Emphasis on traits
	Ecological biology:
	    Holistic
	    Emphasis on processes

Operational Model	

Production model:
    Concerned with economic
        efficiency and productivity
    Emphasis on business growth
        and profits
    Global mass production and
        mass consumption
	Development model:
	    Concerned with social and
	        economic equity
	    Emphasis on household and
	        community welfare
	    Local craft production serving
	        local markets

Organizational Model	

Corporate model:
    large vertically or horizontally
        integrated multinational
        corporations competing in a
        global market
    Ideal form is the large firm
	Community model:
	    Smaller, locally controlled
	        enterprises organized into
	        industrial districts, regional
	        trade associations, producer
	        cooperatives
	    Ideal form is the small firm

Table 5.1. *(continued)*

Class Positions	
Corporate middle class: Positions in corporate hierarchies (e.g., professional, managerial, administrative occupations)	Independent middle class: Independent middle class composed of small-business owners, farmers, self-employed professional workers
Political Processes	
Not communism	Democracy
Food consumers	Food citizens
Power	
Economic and political power are concentrated	Economic and political power are dispersed
Motors for Change	
Human capital	Civic engagement
Social capital	Social movements
Individual actions	

several fundamental organizational and operational differences between the two approaches, apart from the labels that are attached to each.

Neoclassical Economics versus Pragmatism

The terms "neoclassical economics" and "pragmatism" reference bodies of social science theory. Neoclassical economics is concerned with finding the most efficient and "economical" solution to problems. Pragmatism, on the other hand, is guided by the question "what works?" Where neoclassical economics seeks the most efficient solution to a problem regardless of historical context or place, pragmatism advocates seeking the optimal solution that takes into account the historical, cultural, and environmental conditions that frame problems. Both neo-classical economics and pragmatism can serve as blueprints for agricultural development.[26]

When neoclassical economics and pragmatism are applied to issues of agricultural development, they are frequently discussed under the rubric of modernization and sustainability. Modernization efforts, whether at the community, regional, or societal levels, are clearly grounded on the precepts of free market, neoclassical economics.[27] The motor of development in modernization is the market economy. Modernization processes take root and are most successful in those societies that have free markets. According to the modernization scenario, economic globalization is the ultimate and preferred outcome of development. Industrial agriculture, as opposed to civic agriculture, is geared toward producing relatively standardized, uniform, and homogeneous commodities that can be freely traded in the global marketplace.

In contrast to modernization, advocates of civic agriculture shed the straitjacket of economic determinism and look for an explanation of agricultural development that is driven by social processes other than economics. Both Karl Polanyi and Alexis de Tocqueville have provided starting points for inquiries into civic agriculture.[28]

Polanyi offers a perspective in which the "economy" is seen as a mechanism to meet the material needs of a society through a process of interaction between humans and their environment. As a leading Polanyi scholar, Fred Block notes that prior to the industrial revolution, "The pursuit of human livelihood was structured by kinship, by religion, and by other cultural practices that had very little to do with the economizing of scarce resources. This means that models of formal economics in which individuals maximize economic utilities through competitive behavior cannot easily be applied to such societies."[29]

Tocqueville, on the other hand, shows that the norms and values of civic community are embedded in distinctive social structures and practices. In particular, Tocqueville points to civic associations as cornerstones of the civic community. Writing from this perspective, the political scientist Robert Putnam notes that ". . . a dense network of secondary associations both embodies and contributes to effective social collaboration."[30] Milton Esman and Norman Uphoff, development specialists at Cornell University, also relate civic community to development when they report that "a vigorous network of membership organizations is essential to any serious effort to overcome mass poverty under conditions that are likely to prevail in most developing countries. . . . "[31]

In many ways, civic agriculture is the antithesis of free-market, neoclassically based, commodity agriculture. Rather than pursue "rational" self-interest and assume that everyone else will do the same, "citizens in a civic community, though not selfless saints, regard the public domain as more than a battleground for pursuing personal interest."[32]

Production versus Development Frameworks

The free-market model is at heart a "production" model of agricultural development. For farmers and food processors the path to success is clearly spelled out. To be successful, one must focus exclusively on economic efficiency and productivity. Low-cost production becomes not only the "guiding" principle for the economically rational producer; it becomes the "only" principle.[33]

The business strategy for the "production-oriented" commodity farmer focuses on growth and increasing profit margins. Taken to its logical conclusion, globally organized mass production will articulate hand in glove with globally organized mass markets. Consumers in Southeast Asia, Africa, or South America will be confronted with an array of products and services not unlike the array of products presented to consumers in Europe, North America, or Japan. Indeed, in the global marketplace, consumers will demand the same "choices."[34]

The civic agriculture perspective can best be described as representing a "development" model of agriculture and food production. Economic efficiency is but one yardstick by which to measure success or failure. Equity and environmental issues within the community are given weight that is equal to or greater than efficiency and productivity. Decisions are not based solely on what is best for the bottom line. Instead, a broad array of environmental and social factors are brought into the decision-making calculus. The emphasis for producers working out of a civic agriculture framework is on household and community welfare. A keystone of civic agriculture is that a modern and technologically advanced form of agriculture will be tightly woven into markets that serve local consumers.[35]

Experimental Biology versus Ecological Biology

Conventional agriculture is anchored to a scientific paradigm that is rooted in experimental biology. It embodies an approach to farming that focuses on creating and enhancing "favorable" traits of crop varieties and animal species. Further, in a capitalist economic system, the traits (products) developed by genetic engineers are turned into commodities that can be bought, sold, and traded on the world market. As such, the reductionist nature of experimental biology, which identifies/creates "traits," dovetails nicely with the reductionism of neoclassical economics, which provides the framework for turning these traits into "property."

Civic agriculture rests on a biological paradigm best described as "ecological." As such, civic agriculture is not readily amenable to incorporating the techniques/technologies of reductionist science. Ecological approaches to agriculture seek not so much to increase output/yield but to identify and moderate production processes that are "optimal."

Corporate versus Community Orientation

The civic agriculture approach is oriented toward nurturing and sustaining local social and economic systems, while the free-market approach is directed toward beating down local barriers to economic globalization. The desired outcome under the free-market scenario is a global (mass) market that articulates with standardized, low-cost, mass-production enterprises. Sustainable development, on the other hand, rests on production and consumption maintaining at least some economic linkages to the local community.

In the free-market model, the ideal form of production is the large firm. Large firms are able to capture "economies of scale" and hence produce goods more cheaply than smaller, and presumably less efficient, firms. From this perspective, large producers link with large wholesalers, large wholesalers link with large retailers, and large retailers serve the mass market. Large multinational corporations are the driving engines in the development scenario.[36]

The civic community perspective advocates smaller, well-integrated firms cooperating with one another to meet the needs of consumers in local (and occasionally specialty global) markets. The ideal form is the "production district."[37] Firms bound together into production ensembles share information and combine forces to market their products. The state supports this economic venture by ensuring that all firms have access to the same pool of resources such as information, labor, and infrastructure and that policies do not favor one group of producers over another group.

Corporate Middle Class versus Independent Middle Class

From the free-market/modernization perspective, a worker's social class position is part and parcel of the corporate hierarchy. As the corporation goes, so goes the employment prospects of the individual. Not surprisingly, in an economy dominated by large corporations an individual's engagement with the civic affairs of the local community is tempered by his or her allegiance to the corporation. When a choice must be made between what is good for the company and what is good for the community, the company's priorities almost always trump those of the community.[38]

The economically independent middle class is rooted in the local community. As both C. Wright Mills and Melville Ulmer as well as Walter Goldschmidt showed, the independent middle class is more likely to participate in civic affairs and concern itself with finding solutions to local social problems. What is "good" for the socioeconomic health and well-being of the local community is integrally tied to the welfare of the small-business community.[39]

Political Processes and Power

Civic agriculture flourishes in a democratic environment. Problem solving around the social, economic, and environmental issues related to agriculture and food requires that all citizens have a say in how the agriculture and food system is organized. Indeed, citizen participation in agriculture and food-related organizations and associations is a cornerstone of civic agriculture. Through active engagement in the food system, civic agriculture has the potential to transform individuals from passive consumers into active food citizens. A food citizen is someone who has not only a stake but also a voice in how and where his or her food is produced, processed, and sold.[40]

The free-market neoclassical system of conventional agriculture, on the other hand, does not necessarily benefit from democracy and, in fact, may be constrained by the politics put into place through democratic actions of citizens. The political scientist Benjamin Barber recently noted, "Capitalism requires consumers with access to markets; such conditions may or may not be fostered by democracy."[41] Agriculture and food systems organized around "free markets" exist in many nondemocratic countries around the world today. In fact, one would be hard pressed to find many nations in which markets are not used to regulate food production.[42] The freedom of consumers to choose which food products to purchase should not be confused with their freedom to shape the practices or regulate the companies that produce, process, and sell the food.

Motors for Change

The free-market model of agricultural development rests on the belief that the "best" and most "efficient" outcomes are found in a system where individuals are "free" to pursue their own self-interests. It is assumed, of course, that when all the rhetoric is scraped away, self-interested individuals are at heart "capitalists." Human capital, social capital, and technology are the motors for change. Human capital increases the productivity of workers and integrates them tightly into the corporate regime. Social capital provides the environment of trust and cooperation that allows human capital to flourish. Technology extends labor's productivity and through intellectual property rights becomes another tool of corporate control.[43]

From the perspective of civic agriculture, change is generated by social movements and is oriented toward community problem solving. Civically engaged individuals come together in local organizations and associations to solve the problems facing their communities. Shared responsibility for the common good drives the civic community.[44]

Civic Agriculture and Sustainable Agriculture

"Sustainable agriculture" is a term that became popular in the 1980s as an organized response to many of the shortcomings of conventional agriculture. Sustainable agriculture is used to denote a more environmentally sound and socially responsible system of agricultural production than has traditionally existed in most Western societies. While there are many definitions of "sustainable agriculture," one of the more widely accepted definitions was developed by the U.S. Department of Agriculture and published as part of the 1990 Farm Bill. According to the USDA, sustainable agriculture is

> An integrated system of plant and animal production practices having a site-specific application that will, over the long-term: 1) satisfy human food and fiber needs; 2) enhance environmental quality and the natural resource base upon which the agricultural economy depends; 3) make the most efficient use of non-renewable resources and integrate, where appropriate, natural biological cycles and controls; 4) sustain the economic viability of farm operations; and 5) enhance the quality of life for farmers and society as a whole.[45]

It is important to note that this definition encompasses an economic dimension, an environmental dimension, and a social/community dimension. Sustainable agriculture encompasses a set of production practices that are economically profitable for farmers, that preserve and enhance environmental quality, and that contribute to the well-being of farm households while nurturing local community development. Sustainable agriculture denotes a holistic, systems-oriented approach to farming that focuses on the interrelationships of social, economic, and environmental processes.

In an important study of the differences between conventional agriculture and sustainable agriculture, the rural sociologists Curtis Beus and Riley Dunlap identified key elements that distinguish the two agricultural paradigms.[46] Beus and Dunlap's results are summarized in table 5.2. They saw domination of nature versus harmony with nature as one of the key points of difference between the two approaches. Likewise, the reductionist nature of conventional agriculture was captured by the emphasis on commodity specialization, while the problem-solving attribute of sustainable agriculture was aligned with diversity.

The underlying social science paradigms were portrayed by Beus and Dunlap as competition versus community. Conventional agriculture rests on a business orientation, with a primary emphasis on speed, quantity, and profit. The community orientation of sustainable agriculture, on the other hand, rests on cooperation, with an emphasis on permanence, quality, and beauty.

It is not too difficult to see the connections between sustainable agriculture and civic agriculture. Indeed, sustainable agriculture could be seen as a logical antecedent to civic agriculture. The term "civic agriculture" captures the problem-solving foundations of sustainable agriculture. But civic agriculture

Table 5.2. Selected Elements of Conventional Agriculture and
Sustainable Agriculture

Conventional agriculture	Sustainable agriculture
Domination of nature	*Harmony with nature*
Humans are separate from and superior to nature	Humans are part of and subject to nature
Natures consists primarily of resources to be used	Nature is valued primarily for its own sake
Life cycle incomplete; decay (recycling of wastes) neglected	Life cycle complete; growth and decay balanced
Human-made systems imposed on nature	Natural ecosystems are imitated
Production maintained by agricultural chemicals	Production maintained by development of healthy soil
Highly processed, nutrient-fortified food	Minimally processed, naturally nutritious food
Specialization	*Diversity*
Narrow genetic base	Broad genetic base
More plants grown in monocultures	More plants grown in polycultures
Single-cropping in succession	Multiple crops in complementary rotations
Separation of crops and livestock	Integration of crops and livestock
Standardized production systems	Locally adapted production systems
Highly specialized, reductionist science and technology	Interdisciplinary, systems oriented science and technology
Competition	*Community*
Lack of cooperation, self-interest	Increased cooperation
Farm traditions and rural culture outdated	Preservation of farm traditions and rural culture
Small rural communities not necessary to agriculture	Small rural communities essential to agriculture
Farmwork a drudgery; labor input to be minimized	Farmwork rewarding; labor an essential to be made meaningful
Farming is a business only	Farming is a way of life as well as a business
Primary emphasis on speed, quantity, and profit	Primary emphasis on permanence, quality, and beauty

Source: Adapted from Beus and Dunlap, 1990, "Conventional versus Alternative
Agriculture: The Paradigmatic Roots of the Debate."

goes further by referencing the emergence and growth of community-based agriculture and food production activities that not only meet consumer demands for fresh, safe, and locally produced foods but create jobs, encourage entrepreneurship, and strengthen community identity. Civic agriculture brings together production and consumption activities within communities and offers consumers real alternatives to the commodities produced, processed, and marketed by large agribusiness firms.

Why Didn't Small Business Flourish?

If smaller-scale producers, including family farmers, offer more positive social and economic outcomes for rural households and communities, why then did the United States virtually abandon this development path in favor of one in which large agribusiness corporations assumed the dominant role? More to the point, why did policy makers largely ignore the provocative *community-building* findings reported by C. Wright Mills and Melville Ulmer and Walter Goldschmidt in the 1940s and uncritically accept the underlying *community-busting* tenets of the free-market/modernizaton paradigm?

Part of answer may have to do with the historical period in which Goldschmidt and Mills and Ulmer published their findings. Both of these research projects were undertaken at a time when big business had become the primary engine for military production during World War II. Once established, the military industrial complex became a model for large-scale, corporate industrial organization throughout the economy, including agriculture and food production. The consequences of an economy increasingly organized around large-scale economic enterprises for workers and communities were unknown. Coming out of the Second Word War, at least some members of Congress felt compelled to hold hearings on this subject.[47]

While Goldschmidt's and Mills and Ulmer's studies affirmed the social and economic benefits of small business and the family farm for community life, and the deleterious effects of big business and big agribusiness, little, if anything, was done to stem the trend toward economic concentration. Indeed, the decades after World War II were part of an era that the economists Barry Bluestone and Bennett Harrison have called "Pax Americana."[48] According to these authors

> In the years following World War II, a host of public policies promoted and facilitated the centralization and concentration of control over private capital. Especially in the form of tax breaks to business, these political and legal "incentives" were often publicly justified as potential "job creation" devices. But whatever the official rationale, the "de facto" outcome of government policy was to promote and protect concentrated economic power . . . in the United States. . . .[49]

One consequence of the concentration of economic power was that ". . . postwar economic growth . . . promised to generate the material basis for . . . raising workers' standard of living. . . . This wealth in turn made it possible for government to legitimate the new order . . . by greatly expanding the 'social wage': that amalgam of benefits, worker protections, and legal rights that acts to generally increase the social security of the working class."[50] But as Bluestone and Harrison and others[51] correctly noted, as global competition heightened and corporate profits in the United States fell in the 1970s, ". . . the willingness of capital to honor the social contract [with labor] and the ability of the U.S. economy to afford a large and growing safety net would come to an end."[52]

Today we are in the middle of a rapid transformation of our agriculture and food systems. Driven in large part by the imperatives of global capitalism, a handful of large multinational agribusiness firms and food corporations are directly and indirectly shaping how and where food is produced. The outcome of this transformation is likely to be an increasingly homogeneous, uniform, and standardized set of consumer products and a continued erosion of community life. Yet in the push toward globalization, a counter trend toward civic agriculture and a relocalization of at least some production and consumption is evident.

CHAPTER 6

Civic Agriculture and Community Agriculture Development

———⊷✕⊶———

Profiling Civic Agriculture

The industrial type of agriculture produces most of America's food and fiber. However, a new form of civic agriculture that does not fit this conventional model of food production is emerging throughout the country and especially on the East and West Coasts. In this new civic agriculture, local agriculture is being reborn. This trend is most advanced and evident in the Northeast, especially New York, Vermont, and Massachusetts, where small-scale, locally oriented producers and processors have become keys in revitalizing rural areas of the region. These producers represent the vanguard of an important social trend.

To be sure, there is an emerging debate about whether civically organized local food systems can continue to expand and flourish in a globalizing environment. However, over the past ten years, an accumulating body of research has begun to assess the benefits of small enterprises on the level of civic and community welfare. Communities that nurture local systems of agricultural production and food distribution as one part of a broader plan of economic development may gain greater control over their economic destinies, enhance the level of social capital among their residents, and contribute to rising levels of civic welfare and socioeconomic well-being.[1]

Civic agriculturalists and their enterprises are a varied lot, and no one set of characteristics perfectly defines these new producers. However, a profile that captures the tendencies of their operations compared with those of conventional agricultural producers can be constructed (table 6.1). Civic agriculture is oriented toward local market outlets that serve local consumers rather than national or international mass markets. Farmers' markets, roadside stands, U-pick operations, and community-supported agriculture (CSA) are organizational manifestations of civic agriculture. Civic agriculture is seen as an integral part of rural and urban communities, not merely as the production of commodities. The direct contact between civic farmers and consumers nurtures bonds of community. In civic agriculture, producers forge direct links to consumers rather than indirect links through middlemen (wholesalers, brokers, processors, etc.).

Table 6.1. Six Characteristics of Civic Agriculture

(1)	Farming is oriented toward local markets that serve local consumers rather than national or international mass markets.
(2)	Agriculture is seen as an integral part of rural communities, not merely as production of commodities.
(3)	Farmers are concerned more with high quality and value-added products and less with quantity (yield) and least-cost production practices.
(4)	Production at the farm level is often more labor-intensive and land-intensive and less capital-intensive and land-extensive. Farm enterprises tend to be considerably smaller in scale and scope than industrial producers.
(5)	Producers more often rely on local, site-specific knowledge and less on a uniform set of "best management practices."
(6)	Producers forge direct market links to consumers rather than indirect links through middlemen (wholesalers, brokers, processors, etc.).

Farmers engaged in civic agriculture are concerned more with high-quality and value-added products and less with quantity (yield) and least-cost production practices. Civic farmers cater to local tastes and meet the demand for varieties and products that are often unique to a particular region or locality.

Civic agriculture at the farm level is often more labor-intensive and land-intensive and less capital-intensive. Civic farm enterprises tend to be considerably smaller in scale and scope than those of industrial producers. Civic farming is a craft enterprise as opposed to an industrial enterprise. As such, it harks back to the way in which farming was organized in the early part of the twentieth century. Civic agriculture takes up social, economic, and geographic spaces not filled (or passed over) by industrial agriculture.

Civic agriculture often relies on indigenous, site-specific knowledge and less on a uniform set of "best management practices." The industrial model of farming is characterized by homogenization and standardization of production techniques. The embedding of civic agriculture in the community and a concern with environmental conditions fosters a problem-solving perspective that is site-specific and not amenable to a "one size fits all" mentality.[2]

Civic agriculture enterprises are visible in many forms on the local landscape. *Farmers' markets* provide immediate, low-cost, direct contact between local farmers and consumers and are an effective economic development strategy for communities seeking to establish stronger local food systems. *Community* and *school gardens* provide fresh produce to underserved populations, teach food production skills to people of all ages, and contribute to agricultural literacy. *Small-scale farmers,* especially organic producers, across the country have pioneered the development of local marketing systems and formed "production networks" that are akin to manufacturing industrial districts. *Community-supported agriculture* (CSA) operations forge direct links between nonfarm households and their CSA farms. New *grower-controlled marketing cooperatives* are forming, especially in peri-urban areas, to more effectively tap emerging regional markets for locally produced food and agricultural products. *Agricultural districts* organized around particular commodities (such as wine) have served to stabilize farms and farmland in many areas of the country. *Community kitchens* provide the infrastructure and technical expertise necessary to launch new food-based enterprises. *Specialty producers* and *on-farm processors* of products for which there are not well developed mass markets (deer, goat/sheep cheese, free-range chickens, organic dairy products, artisanal cheeses, etc.) and *small-scale, off-farm, local processors* add value in local communities and provide markets for farmers who cannot produce or choose not to produce bulk commodities for the mass market. What these civic agriculture efforts have in common is that they have the potential to nurture local economic development, maintain diversity and quality in products, and provide forums where producers and consumers can come together to solidify bonds of community.

Community-Supported Agriculture

Community-supported agriculture consists of a group of individuals or families who commit resources (money and/or labor) to a farmer and become, in essence, shareholders of the farm.[3] In return for their investment, the shareholders receive part of what the farm produces that season. CSA shareholders provide farmers with the money they need to finance their operations before the growing season begins. In this way, the shareholders incur along with the farmers both the risks and the benefits of food production.

Most CSAs offer their members (shareholders) a variety of fruits, vegetables, herbs, and flowers in season. Some CSAs also produce eggs, milk, meat, baked and canned goods, and even firewood. In a recent study of how CSAs work, Bruno Dyck found that most ranged in size from 35 to 200 shareholders. A typical box of food, usually distributed weekly, one per shareholder, held between five and ten pounds of fruits and vegetables. Consumers pay from $10 to $35 per week, and an average share for a season was $346.[4]

Overall, successful CSAs are successful businesses. They have been able to carve out a segment of the market for fresh, locally produced vegetables that consumers desire. Most CSAs produce some or all of the "top eight" vegetables: corn, lettuce, carrots, tomatoes, green beans, broccoli, onions, and potatoes. The successful CSA uses staggered plantings so that shareholders have a wide variety of fresh food for a long period of time. And every season specialty items like berries and flowers are added to the season's bounty.

Each CSA is organized to meet the needs of its shareholders. CSAs vary according to the level of financial and labor commitments of their members, their decision-making structures, ownership arrangements, and methods of payment and food distribution. Four of the most common forms of CSA include[5]

1. Farmer-directed CSAs: The producer organizes the CSA and takes major responsibility for managing it. Shareholders are seen as "subscribers" and have minimal involvement in the day-to-day operation of the farm. For a cash share, paid before the season begins, subscribers to the farm receive a box of food and other agricultural products on a weekly basis throughout the growing season.

2. Consumer-directed CSAs: A group (community) of consumers organize the CSA and then recruit a farmer to produce for them. Decisions regarding what will be grown and under what methods are made by the consumers, though the farmer is typically brought into these discussions. Labor is sometimes provided by CSA members.

3. Farmer-coordinated CSAs: Two or more producers pool their resources and expertise to produce a wide variety of food and agricultural products for an expanded group of consumers. Farmer-coordinated CSAs might include milk, eggs, and meat in addition to the fruits and vegetables typically associated with CSA operations. Each producer in the coordinated CSA specializes in one product or a set of products. A network of CSA producers thus meets a wider set of needs than any one farmer could individually.

4. Farmer-consumer cooperatives: Producers and consumers join together to purchase land and equipment for the CSA. Decisions regarding what to grow and under what conditions are made jointly by the farmers and the shareholders.

In all four CSA types, the farmer develops a production plan and budget. This is sometimes done with shareholder input and sometimes without it. The budget covers all the anticipated costs of production, including a fair wage for the farmer and other employees of the CSA. The total costs are then divided among the number of shares to be sold. Some CSAs have developed arrangements to subsidize low-income shareholders and to divert part of the food produced to food banks and other emergency food outlets.

Although CSAs take many forms, all are committed to establishing and maintaining a more local and just food system. CSAs combine a concern over land stewardship with an imperative to maintain productive and profitable small farms. In a 1995 study of CSA shareholders, Cynthia Abbott Cone and Ann Kakaliouras found that environmental and community concerns were more important than the price of food as reasons why the shareholders joined a CSA (see table 6.2).[6]

CSAs are an important part of civic agriculture. They strengthen the local food economy and preserve farmland. A web of connected and cooperatively organized CSAs could represent a real and viable alternative to the mass-produced, homogeneous, imported produce found in most supermarkets today.

Table 6.2. Consumer Perspectives on Community-Supported Agriculture

---

 1. Source of organic produce
 2. Source of fresh produce
 3. Concern for a healthy environment
 4. Support for local food sources
 5. Support the small farmer
 6. Knowing how and where their food is grown
 7. Desire to eat vegetables in season
 8. Desire to reduce packaging
 9. Health reasons
10. To participate in community
11. An opportunity to be connected to a piece of land
12. Price
13. Unusual varieties of food
14. A place to bring up children
15. An opportunity to attend festivals and events
16. An opportunity to be around farm animals

Source: Cone and Kakaliouras, 1995, "The Quest for Purity, Stewardship of the Land, and Nostalgia for Sociability: Resocializing Commodities through Community Supported Agriculture."

Restaurant Agriculture

Restaurant agriculture, which is sometimes referred to as "culinary agriculture," involves a production and marketing strategy that brings together farmers and chefs in a mutually supporting and beneficial relationship. Farmers and chefs work together to develop cuisines that draw on the unique aspects of local agriculture. Over the course of a year, chefs who participate in restaurant-supported agriculture often change their menus to incorporate different products as they become available during the growing season.

Farmers who commit to restaurant-supported agriculture provide restaurant owners and chefs high-quality fruits, vegetables, meats, and dairy products. For these consumers, low price is not a major concern.[7] Building trusting relationships between restaurant owners and farmers is the key to success. Maintaining trust requires developing a high degree of familiarity among farmers, chefs, and restaurant owners. Annual visits to one another's businesses are but one way that farmers and chefs come to understand each partner's needs.

Farmers' Markets

Before large supermarkets became a fixture on America's food landscape, farmers' markets provided consumers with a wide array of fresh, local produce. Most cities and towns had at least one farmers' market. In large cities, local farmers' markets catered to the particular tastes and wants of residents who lived in ethnic neighborhoods.

The number of farmers' markets in the United States began to decline in the 1920s with the advent of the modern supermarket. By the 1970s, the number of farmers' markets reached its nadir, with fewer than one hundred still operating. Although the number of farmers' markets plunged, especially after World War II, they never totally disappeared. Like an old idea whose time had come again, farmers' markets began what has become a rather remarkable rebound.[8] The most recent figures from the U.S. Department of Agriculture show over three thousand farmers' markets in 2002. In New York City alone, farmers' markets operate in twenty-eight different locations.

Farmers' markets offer a convenient outlet for producers who cannot or will not develop linkages to the mass market. They also fill an important niche for consumers who value quality, freshness, and variety over quantity and uniformity in the food they purchase. Most farmers' market vendors pride themselves on selling varieties of fruits and vegetables that cannot be found in the typical mass-market grocery store.

While health- and food-conscious consumers are purchasing more fresh fruits and vegetables than ever from farmers' markets, local government officials see farmers' markets as engines of economic and community development. In a survey of 115 farmers' market vendors, we found that farmers' markets provide a venue for three groups of producers. First, for some traditional full-time farmers, farmers' markets can provide a steady source of income. Over the past several decades, the number of marketing alternatives in the processing sector has diminished considerably. The number of small-scale food processors, those most likely to articulate with small farmers, has decreased almost everywhere. For small-scale producers, farmers' markets may represent an economic lifeline.[9]

Part-time growers and market gardeners represent another segment of the agricultural community who benefit from farmers' markets. Farmers' markets allow these producers to sell their products directly to the consumer and can supplement other marketing outlets such as roadside stands, direct-mail marketing, and U-pick operations.

In addition to agricultural producers, farmers' markets serve as outlets for local artisans, craftspeople, and other entrepreneurs. Farmers' markets are low-overhead outlets for handicrafts as well as homemade and farm-based manufactured products. For some entrepreneurs, selling at a farmers' markets is the first step toward beginning a formal business. For others, it is a low-risk way to supplement existing income streams. In either case, farmers' markets serve as a bridge between households, as informally organized production units, and local/community marketplaces.[10]

As social institutions and social organizations, farmers' markets can be important components of civic agriculture. As bridges between the formal and informal sectors of the economy, they enable individual entrepreneurs and their families to contribute to the economic life of their communities by providing goods and services that may not be readily available through formal market channels. They embody what is unique and special about local communities and help to differentiate one community from another.

Roadside Stands

Perhaps the most familiar and ubiquitous form of civic agriculture is the roadside stand. A roadside stand can be considered a micro version of a farmers' market. Because most roadside stands are operated by one farm household, the range of products is generally more limited than one would find at a typical farmers' market. However, roadside stands share many of the organizational and "civic" features of farmers' markets. As in farmers' markets, a wide variation exists in the types of facilities, products, and services associated with farmer-run roadside stands. Some are simply "informal" operations located on remote country roads with a sign stating that one or more agricultural or food items such as eggs, maple syrup, or honey can be obtained at the farmhouse. Others are located in large buildings on major highways and sell a wide variety of fruits, vegetables, food products, and local crafts.[11]

Although roadside stands come in all shapes and sizes, a basic distinction exists between what are termed "producers" and "marketers." Marketers tend to offer broader product lines and produce only a small percentage of the fruits and vegetables they sell. Producers, on the other hand, sell a narrow range of produce, most of which is grown on the farm.

Neither the USDA nor any other branch of the federal government keeps track of the number of roadside stands in the United States. However, a number of states publish the names and addresses of farm stands on an annual basis. For many states, roadside stands are integrated into their tourism efforts. In the mid-1990s, it was estimated that there were over 25,000 roadside stands nationwide. California alone had over 2,000 farm stands, while Ohio had almost 1,000 and Massachusetts reported over 600.[12]

A study prepared for the Ohio Department of Agriculture showed that over 55 percent of Ohio households had shopped at a roadside market. When asked to rate roadside stands against large supermarkets, respondents in the Ohio study found produce quality, produce freshness, and produce prices better at roadside stands than at supermarkets. For households that did not shop at roadside stands, the issue of convenience was given most often as the main reason for not shopping. However, over 80 percent of the nonshoppers said that they would patronize farm stands if they were conveniently located near their homes.[13]

At many roadside stands, up to 90 percent of the patrons are repeat customers. Over time they forge bonds with the producers. Not surprisingly, when the Ohio respondents were asked what influenced their decision to shop at roadside stands, almost 90 percent said that they wished to support local farmers, and 87 percent expressed a desire to buy locally grown produce.[14]

Both roadside stands and farmers' markets typify the growing importance of civic agriculture in the United States. They are places that bring together producers and consumers and allow for meaningful interaction between them. Farmers' markets and farm stands bridge the divide between the local community and the local economy. From a traditional economic perspective, farmers' markets and farm stands may not make good economic sense. From a community perspective, however, they nurture local economic development, maintain diversity and quality in products, and provide opportunities for producers to come together to solidify bonds of local identity and solidarity.

Urban Agriculture, City Farming, Community Gardens

To many people, urban agriculture and city farming sound like oxymorons. Most of our food and agricultural products are produced on farms that are located far from the bright lights of the city. Over the past twenty years, however, farming opportunities have been sprouting in the nation's metropolitan areas.

According to the Canadian bioecologist William Rees, urban agriculture includes growing crops and raising some forms of livestock in or very near cities for local consumption. Community or urban gardens are probably the most visible form of urban agriculture. The first community gardens were organized by the mayor of Detroit in the 1890s to help families cope with the effects of the economic depression of that era. Throughout history, whenever there has been a shortage of food or money, community gardens have flourished. The Liberty and Victory Gardens of World Wars I and II served to supplement the food rationing imposed on the nation at that time. Community gardens also surfaced during the Great Depression as part of the nation's "emergency food system."[15]

Even today, many community gardens are critical sources of food for low-income people. While it costs next to nothing to garden, the average urban garden produces about 540 pounds of food a year. If purchased in a grocery store, the fruits and vegetables grown in the average garden would cost almost $500.[16]

But many community gardens today are more than just sources of almost-free food for poor and low-income people. Many observers have noted that community gardens are a "way for people to work together, socialize and talk with their neighbors. Users plan, construct, and maintain the space, thus building community relations at the same time they save money and lower their cost of living."[17] Urban gardens nurture not only plants and animals but people and their cultures as well.

Urban gardens can teach entrepreneurial skills and spawn and sustain a broad range of new employment opportunities. Not only do community gardens teach horticultural skills, but in some cases they encourage new marketing initiatives, environmental management activities, and community development processes.

Most importantly, William Rees notes that "urban farming can contribute to the rebirth of civil society and development of community as neighbors cooperate in the establishment, management and supervision of community-owned or accessible garden plots . . ."[18] Recently, the *Trends Journal* noted that urban gardening will likely be among the most visible manifestations of a new urban revival—a revival that sees neighborhoods and the groups and organizations embedded in them as the building blocks of a vital civic community.[19]

Measuring Civic Agriculture

Many civic agriculture enterprises exist off the radar screens of most federal and state agencies. Only recently, for example, has the USDA begun collecting and distributing information on farmers' markets.[20] And in 2002, the USDA began an organic certification program. However, it is unclear how many "organic" farmers will actually participate in the National Organic Program, in part because many smaller-scale producers already have a customer base for whom national certification is not needed.[21]

Despite the lack of reliable national statistics on civic agriculture, various organizations around the country have been trying to monitor the growth of civic agriculture. The Community, Food, and Agriculture Program at Cornell University, for example, regularly updates its listing of civic agriculture and food enterprises in New York.[22] Table 6.3 shows that the number of farmers' markets grew from 6 in 1964 to 269 by

Table 6.3. Civic Agriculture Trends in New York State

Types of civic agriculture	No. (year)	No. (year)
Farmers' markets	6 (1964)	269 (2002)
Organic farmers	26 (1988)	290 (2002)
Small wineries	35 (1981)	130 (2002)
Community kitchens	0 (1994)	7 (2000)
Community gardens	550 (1978)	1,500 (2000)
Small-scale food processors	320 (1980)	939 (2001)
Community-supported agriculture (csa)	53 (1993)	80 (2002)
Farms selling direct to public	3,453 (1992)	4,038 (1997)

Source: Community, Food, and Agriculture Program, Cornell University, Ithaca, N.Y.

2002. The number of small-scale organic farmers increased over tenfold between 1988 and 2002, while the number of community gardens increased threefold since 1978. The number of farmers selling directly to the public increased by nearly 600 between 1992 and 1997. Today nearly one in seven farmers in New York sells directly to the public.

Civic agriculture activities such as urban gardens, farmers' markets, roadside stands, and CSAs, as aspects of the civic community, become a powerful template around which to build non- or extramarket relationships between persons, social groups, and institutions that have been distanced from each other. Indeed a growing number of community groups across the United States are recognizing that creative new forms of community development, built around the regeneration of local food systems, may eventually generate sufficient economic and political power to mute the more socially and environmentally destructive manifestations of the global marketplace. A turn toward a more civic agriculture is both theoretically and practically possible. Indeed, the seeds have been sown and are taking root throughout the United States. Civic agriculture represents a promising economic alternative that can nurture community businesses, save farms, and preserve farmland by providing consumers with fresh, locally produced agricultural and food products.

CHAPTER 7

From Commodity Agriculture to Civic Agriculture

━━◆━◆━━

Commodity Agriculture

As American agriculture turns down the path of a new century, we see that the independent, self-reliant farmer of the last century is rapidly disappearing from the rural landscape. Farmers, who were once the backbone of the rural economy, have been reduced to mere cogs in a well-oiled agribusiness machine. The real value in agriculture no longer rests in the commodities produced by farmers, but instead is captured by the corporately controlled and integrated sectors of the agri-food system that bracket producers with high-priced inputs on one side and tightly managed production contracts and marketing schemes on the other side.

The prime supporters of current agricultural policy in the United States have been the land grant colleges and universities, the U.S. Department of Agriculture, and more recently large, multinational agribusiness firms. The land-grant system was organized to bring the methods of scientific research to agriculture.[1] At U.S. land-grant universities, the emphasis in the classroom and research laboratory has been on *commodity production*. As different production-oriented agricultural disciplines were formed over the past 120 years such as agronomy, plant pathology, the animal sciences, plant breeding, and entomology, they broke apart "farming" bit by bit into disciplinary niches.

The goals were the same, however, across disciplines. In the plant sciences, attention was directed at increasing commodity yields by enhancing soil fertility, reducing pests, and developing new genetic varieties. Animal scientists, on the other hand, focused on health, nutrition, and breeding. The scientific and technological advances wrought by land-grant scientists were filtered through a farm management paradigm in agricultural economics that championed sets of "best management practices" as the policy blueprints for successful and presumably profitable operations.[2]

Agricultural policy at the national and state levels focuses primarily on commodities as units of observation, analysis, experimentation, and intervention. Farmers and farms have largely been overlooked by policy makers. Indeed, farmers are often reduced to *workers* whose primary tasks are to follow production procedures outlined from above. And farms are simply *places* where production occurs, devoid of connections to the local community or social order.[3]

Commodity agriculture has become synonymous with industrial agriculture. Many of the basic commodities that undergird the U.S. food system are produced on very large farms that are tied to large agribusiness firms through production contracts. Production contracts are especially prevalent among poultry and livestock farms.[4]

The entire system of commodity production is being propped up by large government subsidies. These subsidies favor some producers over others (usually large ones over small ones) and certain production practices over others (usually capital-intensive over organic). A recent report by Brian Riedl of the Heritage Foundation noted that "growers of corn, wheat, cotton, soybeans, and rice receive more than 90 percent of all farm subsidies, while growers of most of the 400 other domestic crops are completely shut out of farm subsidy programs." The report continued: "farm subsidies in 2001 were distributed overwhelmingly to large growers and agribusiness, including a number of Fortune 500 companies. . . . The top 10 percent of recipients—most of whom earn over $250,000 annually—received 73 percent of all farm subsidies in 2001."[5]

The shortcomings of a corporately controlled and managed food system have been revealed in many scholarly books and journal articles, as well as in the popular press.[6] However, only recently has a civic agriculture paradigm emerged to challenge the wisdom of conventional commodity agriculture. The emerging civic approach is associated with a relocalizing of production. From this perspective, agriculture and food endeavors are seen as engines of local economic development and integrally related to the social and cultural fabric of the community.

Refashioning Farming to Fit the Marketplace

Civic agriculture brings together production and consumption activities within communities and offers consumers real alternatives to the commodities produced, processed, and marketed by large agribusiness firms. Civic agriculture is the embedding of local agricultural and food production in the community.[7] Civic agriculture is not only a source of family income for the farmer and food processor; civic agricultural enterprises also contribute to the health and vitality of their local communities in a variety of social, economic, political, and cultural contexts. For example, civic agriculture increases agricultural literacy by directly linking consumers to producers.

Likewise, civic agricultural enterprises have a much higher local economic multiplier than farms or processors that are producing for the global mass market. This means that money spent for civic products stays longer in the local community and is circulated among a wider range of individuals than are dollars spent for imported food produced by large corporations and sold in large supermarkets.

Civic agriculture is a locally organized system of agriculture and food production characterized by networks of producers who are bound together by place. Civic agriculture embodies a commitment to developing and strengthening an economically, environmentally, and socially sustainable agriculture and food production system that relies on local resources and serves local markets and consumers. The imperative to earn a profit is filtered through a set of cooperative and mutually supporting social relations. Community problem solving rather than individual competition is the foundation of civic agriculture.

In order to effect a shift to civic agriculture, it is critical that we recognize and address the fact that control of today's food system rests primarily with powerful and highly concentrated economic interests, and not with local communities or even government. Large-scale, well-managed, capital-intensive, technologically sophisticated, industrial-like operations have become tightly tied into a network of national and global food producers. These farms produce large quantities of highly standardized bulk commodities that are fed into large national and multinational integrators and processors. A few thousand very large farms account for most of the gross agricultural sales, but not necessarily farm income, for farm income is propped up by billions of dollars in farm subsidies. And the current political climate for agriculture, one that endorses biotechnology, free markets, global trade, and the growth of multinational corporations, is likely to make a change toward civic agriculture difficult.

Reconnecting Farm, Food, and Community: Tools for Change

While corporate interests are likely to continue to influence the food system in the direction of increased economic globalization, I believe that communities, organizations, local governments, and even individuals have many tools that can be used to begin to effect change and move toward a more civic agriculture. A new *social blueprint* for agriculture will come from below, not above. Civic engagement with the food system is taking place throughout the country as citizens and organizations grapple with providing food for the hungry, establishing community-based food businesses, and organizing food policy councils. Policies and programs at the local level that support the development of farmers' markets, CSAs, organic production, agricultural districts, community kitchens, community gardens, and all sorts of direct marketing and on-farm processing will foster a more community-friendly and sustainable system of production and consumption. While diverse, these efforts have one thing in common: they are all local problem-solving activities organized around agriculture and food.

Communities can provide alternatives to the products of the global food system only if they develop the necessary infrastructure, maintain an adequate farmland base, and provide sufficient technical expertise so that farmers and processors can successfully compete in the local marketplace against the highly industrialized, internationally organized corporate food system. There is accumulating evidence that civic agriculture is emerging in those U.S. regions that have been hit hard by global competition. Many communities have already begun relocalizing parts of their food and agriculture systems.[8]

There is considerable room for local and state-level policy makers to operate and reinvent an alternative and more community-oriented food and agriculture system virtually everywhere. Already we are seeing the emergence and growth of social movements around local agriculture and food systems. Communities committed to civic agriculture are (1) encouraging local economic development efforts to support community-based food-processing activities; (2) fostering land use policies that protect active farm areas from random residential development; (3) enacting and enforcing zoning codes that allocate land into areas of nonfarm development, areas of natural preservation, and areas for agricultural production; (4) instituting institutional food acquisition practices that integrate local food production directly into the community: and (5) developing educational programs to increase agricultural literacy among both children and adults including school and community gardens, summer internship programs, and community-farm days.[9] An effective agricultural development strategy for civic communities should be geared toward fostering problem solving. Policies to promote and strengthen regional trade associations, local agricultural districts, producer cooperatives, and other forms of locally based economic activity should be part and parcel of a comprehensive community-based agricultural development strategy. Communities would do well not to cede control of their agricultural sector to large, export-oriented, commodity farms and not to rely solely on big-box supermarkets for their food.

Civic Agriculture: Moving from the
Marketplace to the Community

Over the past ten years, an accumulating body of research has begun to assess the benefits of smaller-scale enterprises on the level of civic and community welfare in the United States and elsewhere.[10] Research results suggest that there may be many positive benefits to communities that embrace a *community capitalism* model of economic development.[11] Communities that nurture local systems of agricultural production and food marketing, as one part of a broader plan of diversified economic development, can gain greater control over their economic destinies. They can also enhance the level of civic engagement among their residents, contribute to rising levels of civic welfare and socioeconomic well-being, revitalize rural landscapes, improve environmental quality, and, ultimately, promote long-term sustainability.[12]

Civic agriculture, then, as one aspect of the civic community, becomes a powerful template around which to build non- or extramarket relationships between persons, social groups, and institutions that have been distanced from each other. Indeed a growing number of practitioners and academics across the United States are recognizing that creative new forms of community development, built around the regeneration of local food systems, may eventually generate sufficient economic and political power to mute the more socially and environmentally destructive manifestations of the global marketplace.[13] A turn toward a more civic agriculture is both theoretically and practically possible. Indeed, the seeds have been sown and are taking root throughout the United States.

NOTES

Chapter 1. Introduction: Community Agriculture and Local
Food Systems (pp. 1–7)

1. See Drabenstott 1999, "New Futures for Rural America: The Role for Land-Grant Universities." Two books that describe the changing structure of American agriculture are Gardner 2002, *American Agriculture in the Twentieth Century: How It Flourished and What It Cost,* and Fitzgerald 2003, *Every Farm a Factory: The Industrial Ideal in American Agriculture.* Buttel, Larson, and Gillespie 1990, *The Sociology of Agriculture,* is another valuable source.

2. See the work of William Friedland, especially "The New Globalization: The Case of Fresh Produce," 1994. An excellent overview of the local and global dimensions of the food system is presented in Norberg-Hodge, Merrifield, and Gorelick 2000, "Bringing the Food Economy Home."

3. Any comprehensive farm management textbook describes the production function and will discuss its underlying assumptions. See, for example, Kay 1986, *Farm Management: Planning, Control, and Implementation.*

4. Lyson and Raymer have examined interlocking corporate directorates among the ten largest food-processing corporations in the United States. See Lyson and Raymer 2000, "Stalking the Wily Multinational: Power and Control in the U.S. Food System."

5. An early attempt to understand how large cities feed themselves was provided by Walter Hedden in 1929. Hedden coined the term "foodshed" to describe the geographic boundaries of a city's food supply. See Hedden 1929, *How Great Cities Are Fed.*

Chapter 2. From Subsistence to Production (pp. 8–29)

1. See Kolb and de S. Brunner 1940, *A Study of Rural Society: Its Organization and Changes,* p. 46.
2. I computed these figures from data in the 1870 U.S. Census of Population.
3. See Douglas Harper 2001, *Changing Works: Visions of a Lost Agriculture.* Harper is a visual sociologist who has documented how dairy farming in the Northeast changed from a community-centered enterprise in the early part of the twentieth century to an industrially organized commodity-centered enterprise today. He uses photos from the Standard Oil archive and his own work to illustrate these changes.
4. See Robinson and Briggs 1991, "The Rise of Factories in Nineteenth-Century Indianapolis."
5. See United States Census Office 1872, *A Compendium of the Ninth Census.*
6. Karl Polanyi 1944, in *The Great Transformation,* notes the importance of redistribution and reciprocity as organizing principles for the economy prior to the industrial revolution.
7. For a discussion of craft production and mass production see Piore and Sabel 1984, *The Second Industrial Divide.*
8. Ibid., p. 160.
9. Robinson and Briggs 1991, p. 650.
10. Piore and Sabel 1984, p. 20.
11. Fordism and Taylorism represent the organizational and management dimensions of modern mass production. See Linda Lobao 1990, *Locality and Inequality,* for a discussion of Fordism.
12. Many rural communities built lyceum halls to house the traveling chautauquas. Chautauquas are a system of home study; they were popular after the Civil War and often included a summer school. For a discussion of the chautauqua movement see Gould 1961, *The Chautauqua Movement: An Episode in the Continuing American Revolution.*
13. Many books and monographs describe the land-grant college system. See, for example, Nevins 1962, *The Origins of the Land-Grant Colleges and State Universities: A Brief Account of the Morrill Act of 1862 and Its Results,* and the National

Association of State Universities and Land-Grant Colleges 1995, *The Land-Grant Tradition*.

14. The obstacles that prevented farming from following the path of manufacturing toward mass production are outlined in Mann and Dickinson 1978, "Obstacles to the Development of a Capitalist Agriculture." For a counter view see Mooney 1982, "Labor Time, Production Time, and Capitalist Development in Agriculture: A Reconsideration of the Mann-Dickinson Thesis."

15. For a discussion of how farmers viewed the introduction of scientific techniques into farming see Taylor and Jones 1964, *Rural Life and Urbanized Society*, p. 384.

16. Jeffers 1916, "How the Investigator in Farm Management Problems Can Help the Farmer," p. 7.

17. Although modern farm management techniques have decontextualized the farm and farmer from his/her local community, early agricultural economists saw the importance of community. George Warren, an agricultural economist at Cornell University, writing in 1914 put it this way: "There is much to learn about farming in any community that one man cannot hope to learn it alone. The experience of the community is of the utmost value to every farmer. Few farmers realize how much they owe to their neighbors." See Warren 1914, *Farm Management*, p. 98. It was only after World War II that modern farm management took hold and the importance of community and neighbors faded.

18. Brand 1914, *Marketing*, p. 85.

19. The concept of the agricultural treadmill is presented in chapter 5 of Cochrane 1958, *Farm Prices: Myths and Reality*.

20. One of the first books to critically examine the production practices of American agriculture was an edited volume by Richard Merrill, *Radical Agriculture*, 1971. The discussion of chemical use in agriculture is Merrill 1971, "Toward a Self-Sustaining Agriculture."

21. The literature on the social, economic, and environmental effects of agricultural biotechnologies is voluminous and growing. A few sources that will provide an entry into the literature include Evenson, Santaniello, and, Zilberman 2002, *Economic and Social Issues in Agricultural Biotechnology*; Shelton 2002, *Agricultural Biotechnology: Informing the Dialogue*, and Krimsky and

Wrubel 1996, *Agricultural Biotechnology and the Environment: Science, Policy, and Social Issues.*

22. "Occupation" and "industry" are terms used by the U.S. Census Bureau to classify and keep track of the nation's economic activities. For a discussion of the census categories see Anderson 1988, *American Census: A Social History.*

23. See Bromley 1978, "Organization, Regulation, and Exploitation in the So-called 'Urban Informal Sector': The Street Traders of Cali, Colombia," and Moser 1978, "Informal Sector or Petty Commodity Production: Dualism or Dependence in Urban Development."

24. One of the classic models of economic development was proposed by W. W. Rostow 1975, *How It All Began: Origins of the Modern Economy.*

25. For a general discussion of economic development on a global scale see McMichael 1996, *Development and Social Change.*

26. Some of the first sociologists to write about the informal economy in the United States include Castells and Portes 1989, "World Underneath: The Origins, Dynamics, and Effects of the Informal Economy"; Pahl and Wallace 1985, "Household Work Strategies in Economic Recession"; and Sassen-Koob 1989, "New York City's Informal Economy."

27. A history of New York's community gardens can be found in Ferguson 1999, "A Brief History of Grassroots Greening in NYC." A more general treatment of community gardens can be found in Sommers 1984, *The Community Garden Book: New Directions for Creating and Managing Neighborhood Food Gardens in Your Town.*

28. Two notable exceptions to the neglect of the informal economy in rural areas are Jensen, Cornwell, and Findeis 1995, "Informal Work in Nonmetropolitan Pennsylvania," and Tickamyer and Wood 1998, "Identifying Participation in the Informal Economy Using Survey Research Methods."

29. Two books that make this point include Kramer 1987, *Three Farms,* and Schwartz 1992, *Waucoma Twilight: Generations of the Farm.*

30. Schwartz 1992, p. 121.

31. The sustainable-agriculture movement in the United States is about twenty years old. What began as an interest in organic farming has expanded to include a social and economic dimension as well. Three periodicals that deal with sustainable agriculture issues include the *Journal of Sustainable Agriculture, American Journal of Alternative Agriculture,* and *Agriculture and Human Values.*

Chapter 3. Going Global (pp. 30–47)

1. Lehman and Krebs 1996, "Control of the World's Food Supply."
2. These national trends also play out within individual states; see, for example, Lyson 1999, "From Plow to Plate: The Transformation of New York's Food and Agricultural System since 1910."
3. Lyson and Geisler 1992, "Toward a Second Agricultural Divide: The Restructuring of American Agriculture."
4. For a good overview of industrial agriculture in California see Stoll 1998, *The Fruits of Natural Advantage: Making the Industrial Countryside in California.*
5. For an evaluation of the Freedom to Farm Act see Frydenlund 2002, "The Erosion of Freedom to Farm."
6. Stoll 1998.
7. Kneen 1993, *From Land to Mouth: Understanding the Food System,* p. 37.
8. For a discussion on the future of the food system see Gussow 1991, *Chicken Little, Tomato Sauce, and Agriculture: Who Will Produce Tomorrow's Food?*
9. Hamm 1993, "The Potential for a Localized Food Supply in New Jersey."
10. For a discussion of the role of farmland in a global food system see Lyson, Geisler, and Schlough 1998, "Preserving Community Agriculture in a Global Economy."
11. Munton 1992, "Factors of Production in Modern Agriculture," p. 61.
12. Mann and Dickinson 1978.

13. Albrecht and Murdock 1990, *The Sociology of U.S. Agriculture: An Ecological Perspective,* p. 56. California farmers solved the labor problem by drawing on a contingent migrant labor force composed of many different ethnic groups.
14. For a discussion of agricultural labor and problems associated with counting farmworkers see Mehta 2000, *Findings from the National Agricultural Workers Survey (NAWS) 1997-1998: A Demographic and Employment Profile of United States Farmworkers.*
15. Welsh 1996, *The Industrial Reorganization of U.S. Agriculture,* p. 20.
16. Hart 1992, "Marketing Agricultural Produce."
17. Drabenstott 1999.
18. Ibid.
19. Northeast Dairy Business 1999, "Market Gorilla," p. 11.
20. Drabenstott 1999.

Chapter 4. The Global Supply Chain (pp. 48-60)

1. Heffernan 1999, *Consolidation in the Food and Agriculture System.*
2. Ibid.
3. Rural Advancement Foundation International 1999, "The Gene Giants: Masters of the Universe." The Rural Advancement Foundation International (RAFI) recently changed its name to *etcgroup.* Its research and publications can be found at http://www.etcgroup.org.
4. Hart 1992.
5. A history of the Green Giant Company until 1979 is provided by Bengston 1991, *A History of the Green Giant Company, 1903-1979.*
6. Ibid., p. 227.
7. Wentz 1992, "How Martin Sees Grand Met's Global Role."
8. See http://www.Senecafoods.com/Mainpage.html.
9. Kaufman 2000, "Consolidation in Food Retailing: Prospects for Consumers and Grocery Suppliers," p. 21.

10. Ibid. See also Kaufman 2000, "Grocery Retailers Demonstrate Urge to Merge."
11. Lyson and Raymer 2000.
12. Mills 1956, *The Power Elite,* and Domhoff 1983, *Who Rules America Now? A View for the '80s.*
13. Hill 1995, "The Social Organization of Boards of Directors," p. 250.
14. Domhoff 1983, p. 77.
15. Gatlin 1999, "Frito-Lay Shuts Down Marlboro Plant."
16. Patch 1995, *Plant Closings and Employment Loss in Manufacturing.*
17. See, for example, Bellenir 1999, *Diet and Nutrition Sourcebook,* and Sonberg 1995, *The Health and Nutrient Bible.*
18. Pepsico 2003, *2003 Pepsico Annual Report, Pepsico Factbook.*
19. For a general discussion of corporate reach within the food system see Bruno 1992, "The Corporate Capture of the Earth Summit"; Krebs 1992, *The Corporate Reapers,* pp. 289–299, and Ritchie 1993, "NAFTA's Grim Harvest, Free Trade and Sustainable Agriculture."
20. Azzam, Lopez, and Lopez 2002, *Imperfect Competition and Total Factor Productivity Growth in U.S. Food Processing.*
21. The share of economic activity in agriculture accounted for by farmers, input suppliers, and marketers was computed by the agricultural economist Stewart Smith when he was at the University of Maine. It is an often-cited statistic. See Smith 1992, "'Farming'—It's Declining in the U.S."
22. Schlosser 2001, *Fast Food Nation,* p. 8.
23. For a discussion of large dry-lot dairies see Gilbert and Akor 1988, "Increasing Structural Divergence in U.S. Dairying: California and Wisconsin since 1950." For a comprehensive treatment of the industrialization of the livestock sector see Hinrichs and Welsh 2003, "The Effects of the Industrialization of U.S. Livestock Agriculture on Promoting Sustainable Production Practices." See also Welsh 2003, "Agro-food System Restructuring and the Geographic Concentration of U.S. Swine Production."
24. The Internet has many sites devoted to food and agriculture issues. Not only do all the major food and agribusiness companies

maintain Web sites, but a wide range of public interest Web sites can also be found. The site at www.factoryfarming.com is run by the Farm Sanctuary, which is a U.S.-based organization devoted to animal welfare issues. Its headquarters is in Watkins Glen, New York.

25. Heffernan 1999.

Chapter 5. Toward a Civic Agriculture (pp. 61–83)

1. Lyson 2000, "Moving toward Civic Agriculture."
2. DeLind 2002. "Place, Work, and Civic Agriculture: Fields for Cultivation."
3. Some good examples of civic agriculture enterprises can be found in Green and Hilchey 2002, *Growing Home: A Guide to Reconnecting Agriculture, Food, and Communities.*
4. A search of the National Agriculture Library yielded hundreds of books with the title *Farm Management.* Almost all of the books treat the farmer as a rational, economically motivated problem solver.
5. For a contemporary treatment of community problem solving see Young 1999, *Small Towns in Multilevel Society.*
6. Mills and Ulmer 1946, *Small Business and Civic Welfare.* This study was reprinted in Aiken and Mott 1970, *The Structure of Community Power.*
7. Mills and Ulmer did not divulge the names of the six cities they studied in their report. However, by triangulation and reassessing their original data, Lynn Ryan MacKenzie was able to identify the cities. The matched pairs were Grand Rapids, Michigan, and Flint, Michigan; Kalamazoo, Michigan, and Dearborn, Michigan; and Rome, New York, and Nashua, New Hampshire. See MacKenzie 1994, "Capitalism, Power, and Community Well-being: Developing a Model for Understanding the Effect of Local Economic Configuration on Cities and Their Citizens."
8. Cited in Mills and Ulmer 1946, p. v.
9. Ibid., p. 22.
10. Ibid., p. 3.
11. Ibid., pp. 22–23.

12. Goldschmidt 1946, *Small Business and the Community*. This study was reprinted as Goldschmidt 1978, *As You Sow.*
13. Goldschmidt 1978, p. 393.
14. Ibid., p. 395.
15. Ibid., pp. 415–416.
16. Ibid., p. 284.
17. Ibid., pp. 200–201.
18. See Barham 2003, "Translating Terroir: The Global Challenge of French AOC Labeling."
19. Zeitlin 1989, "Introduction," p. 370.
20. Sabel 1993, "Studied Trust: Building New Forms of Cooperation in a Volatile Economy."
21. Perrow 1993, "Small Firm Networks," p. 298.
22. For background material related to the civic community approach see Putnam 1993, *Making Democracy Work;* Barber 1995, *Jihad vs. McWorld;* and Tolbert, Lyson, and Irwin 1998, "Local Capitalism, Civic Engagement, and Socioeconomic Well-being."
23. Irwin, Tolbert, and Lyson 1997, "How to Build Strong Towns."
24. Piore and Sabel 1984, and Bagnasco and Sabel 1995, *Small and Medium Size Enterprises.*
25. Barber 1995.
26. Interest in pragmatism appears to be increasing among social scientists. It is claimed that pragmatism is the only uniquely American social theory. For an early take on pragmatism by a prominent sociologist see Mills 1964, *Sociology and Pragmatism: The Higher Learning in America.* A useful Web site is http://www.pragmatism.org.
27. See, for example, Inkeles 1966, *The Modernization of Man,* and Ingelhart 1997, *Modernization and Postmodernization: Cultural, Economic, and Political Change in 43 Societies.*
28. Polanyi 1944 and Tocqueville 1836, *Democracy in America.*
29. Block 1990, *Postindustrial Possibilities,* p. 39.
30. Putnam 1993, p. 90.
31. Esman and Uphoff 1984, *Local Organizations: Intermediaries in Rural Development,* p. 40.
32. Putnam 1993, p. 88.
33. A number of books written in the last twenty-five years make this point and link it to the deindustrialization of large parts of

the United States. See, for example, Bowles, Gordon, and Weis-kopf 1983, *Beyond the Wasteland;* Korten 1995, *When Corporations Rule the World;* and Mander and Goldsmith 1996, *The Case against the Global Economy.*

34. Barber, 1995.
35. For a description of the possibilities of a more locally organized economy see Shuman 1998, *Going Local: Creating Self-reliant Communities in a Global Age.*
36. McMichael 1996.
37. Piore and Sabel 1984.
38. The emergence of a corporate-oriented economy has attracted attention since at least the 1950s. For a early views on this phenomenon see Mills 1951, *White Collar: The American Middle Classes,* and Whyte 1956, *The Organization Man.*
39. Goldschmidt 1978, and Mills and Ulmer 1946.
40. See Goodman and DuPuis 2002, "Knowing Food and Growing Food: Beyond the Production-Consumption Debate in the Sociology of Agriculture."
41. Barber 1995, p. 15.
42. North Korea is perhaps the one country that has failed to adopt a market-based system of agriculture. Even Cuba has opened up large segments of its agricultural economy to markets.
43. For a discussion of the different types of capital see Flora 1995, "Social Capital and Sustainability: Agriculture and Communities in the Great Plains and the Corn Belt," and Flora et al. 1997, "Entrepreneurial Social Infrastructure and Locally Initiated Economic Development."
44. Young 1999.
45. Food, Agriculture, Conservation, and Trade Act of 1990 (FACTA), Public Law 101–624, Title XVI, Subtitle A, Section 1603 (Washington, D.C.: Government Printing Office, 1990).
46. Beus and Dunlap 1990, "Conventional versus Alternative Agriculture: The Paradigmatic Roots of the Debate."
47. The U.S. Congress was aware of the problems facing small businesses at the end of World War II. It held hearings to assess the situation and also commissioned the 1946 studies by Goldschmidt and by Mills and Ulmer. See "Report of the Smaller War Plants Corporation to the Special Committee to Study Problems

of American Small Business," Document 135, U.S. Senate, 79th Congress, 2nd session.

48. For a discussion of the Pax Americana period see Bluestone and Harrison 1982, *The Deindustrialization of America.*

49. Ibid., p. 126.

50. Ibid., p. 132.

51. See also Bowles, Gordon, and Weiskopf 1983.

52. Bluestone and Harrison 1982, p. 139.

Chapter 6. Civic Agriculture and Community Agriculture Development (pp. 84–98)

1. Green and Hilchey 2002. See also Lyson and Green 1999, "The Agricultural Marketscape: A Framework for Sustaining Agriculture and Communities in the Northeast."

2. Civic agriculture should be viewed as an ideal type. Ideal types are mental constructs against which empirical cases can be compared. The characteristics of the ideal type of civic agriculture were drawn from a number of sources including Wilkins 1995, "Seasonal and Local Diets: Consumers' Role in Achieving a Sustainable Food System"; Center for Rural Affairs 1988, "Agriculture: A Foundation for Rural Economic Development"; Waters 1990, "The Farm—Restaurant Connection"; Bird, Bultena, and Gardner 1995, *Planting the Future;* Kloppenburg 1991, "Social Theory and the De/reconstruction of Agricultural Science: Local Knowledge for an Alternative Agriculture"; Kneen 1993; Johnston and Bryant 1987, "Agricultural Adaptation: The Prospects for Sustaining Agriculture Near Cities"; and Lyson, Gillespie, and Hilchey 1995, "Farmers' Markets and the Local Community: Bridging the Formal and Informal Economy."

3. For background on community supported agriculture see Fieldhouse 1996, "Community Shared Agriculture"; Cone, Myhre, and Grey 2000, "Community-Supported Agriculture: A Sustainable Alternative to Industrial Agriculture?" and Kittredge 1996, "Community Supported Agriculture: Rediscovering Community."

4. Dyck 1992, "Inside the Food System: How Do Community Supported Farms Work?"

5. Appropriate Technology Transfer for Rural Areas (ATTRA) is an excellent source of practical information on CSAs. See, for example, Greer 1999, *Community Supported Agriculture.*

6. Cone and Kakaliouras 1995, "The Quest for Purity, Stewardship of the Land, and Nostalgia for Socialability: Resocializing Commodities through Community Supported Agriculture."

7. Restaurant-supported agriculture (RSA) is a relatively recent phenomenon. Only a few studies have begun to examine the potential economic and social impacts of RSA. The following are useful places to learn more about RSA. ATTRA, www.attra.org/attra-pub/altmeat.html; Berkshire Grown, www.berkshiregrown.com; and Chef's Collaborative, www.chefnet.com/cc2000. See also Green and Hilchey 2002.

8. For some background information on farmers' markets see Lyson, Gillespie, and Hilchey 1995. A good empirical study of farmers' markets is Hughes and Mattson 1992, *Farmers' Markets in Kansas: A Profile of Vendors and Market Organization.*

9. See references in note 8 above. See also Hilchey, Lyson, and Gillespie 1995, *Farmers' Markets and Rural Economic Development.*

10. Lyson, Gillespie, and Hilchey 1995.

11. Hemlick 1991, "Agriculture Adapts to Urbanization: Linking Agriculture to the Economy."

12. Rhodus, Schwartz, and Hoskins 1994, "Ohio Consumer Opinions of Roadside Markets and Farmers' Markets."

13. Ibid.

14. Ibid.

15. Rees 1997, "Why Urban Agriculture?" and Woodsworth 1995, "Community Gardening: A Vancouver Perspective."

16. Woodsworth, 1995.

17. The American Community Garden Association is an important source of information about urban gardens, community gardens, and school gardens: see http://www.communitygarden.org. The quote is from "Comprehensive Plans, Zoning Regulations, and Goals Concerning Community Gardens and Open Green Space from the Cities of Seattle, Berkeley, Boston, and Chicago" on the American Community Garden Web site.

18. Rees 1997.

19. *Trends Journal* 1997 as cited in *Yes!* 1997, "Top Trends '97."

20. Information on farmers' markets can be found at http://www. ams.usda.gov/farmersmarkets/.
21. The National Organic Program home page is at http://www. ams.usda.gov/nop/indexIE.htm.
22. The Community, Food, and Agriculture Program (CFAP) was founded in 1985 as the Farming Alternatives Program. CFAP works with agriculture and food producers and community partners to promote food and agriculture systems that sustain and strengthen farm families, local communities, and natural resources. See http://www.cfap.org.

Chapter 7. From Commodity Agriculture to Civic Agriculture (pp. 99–105)

1. Fisher and Zuiches 1994, "Challenges Confronting Agricultural Research at Land Grant Universities."
2. Kadlec 1985, *Farm Management: Decisions, Operation, Control.*
3. Kay 1986.
4. Welsh 1997, "Vertical Coordination, Producer Response, and the Locus of Control over Agricultural Production Decisions."
5. Riedl 2002, *Still at the Federal Trough: Farm Subsidies for the Rich and Famous Shattered Records in 2001.*
6. An early take on corporate agriculture is Merrill 1976, *Radical Agriculture.* More recent works include Krebs 1992 and Heffernan 1999. See also The Corporate Agribusiness Research Project at http://www.electricarrow.com/CARP/.
7. For a discussion of food system localization see Hinrichs 2003, "The Practice and Politics of Food System Localization."
8. Green and Hilchey 2002.
9. Ibid.
10. Shuman 1998.
11. For a discussion of community capitalism see Tolbert, Lyson, and Irwin 1998.
12. Berry 1996, "Conserving Communities."
13. Kloppenburg, Hendrickson, and Stevenson 1996, "Coming into the Foodshed."

BIBLIOGRAPHY

Aiken, Michael, and Paul E. Mott. 1970. *The Structure of Community Power*. New York: Random House.

Albrecht, Don E., and Steve H. Murdock. 1990. *The Sociology of U.S. Agriculture: An Ecological Perspective*. Ames: Iowa State University Press.

Anderson, Margo J. 1988. *American Census: A Social History*. New Haven, Conn.: Yale University Press.

Azzam, Azzeddine M., Elena Lopez, and Rigoberto A. Lopez. 2002. *Imperfect Competition and Total Factor Productivity Growth in U.S. Food Processing*. Food Marketing Policy Center, Research Report No. 68. Storrs: University of Connecticut, Department of Agricultural and Resource Economics.

Bagnasco, Arnaldo, and Charles F. Sabel. 1995. *Small and Medium Size Enterprises*. London: Pinter.

Barber, Benjamin R. 1995. *Jihad vs. McWorld*. New York: Times Books.

Barham, Elizabeth. 2003. "Translating Terroir: The Global Challenge of French AOC Labeling." *Journal of Rural Studies* 19:127–138.

Bellenir, Karen. 1999. *Diet and Nutrition Sourcebook*. Detroit: Omnigraphics.

Bengston, Roger E. 1991. "A History of the Green Giant Company, 1903–1979." Ph.D. dissertation, University of Minnesota.

Berry, Wendell. 1996. "Conserving Communities." Pp. 407–418 in J. Mander and E. Goldsmith, eds., *The Case against the Global Economy*. San Francisco: Sierra Club Books.

Beus, Curtis E., and Riley E. Dunlap. 1990. "Conventional versus Alternative Agriculture: The Paradigmatic Roots of the Debate." *Rural Sociology* 55:590–616.

Bird, Elizabeth A. R., Gordon L. Bultena, and John C. Gardner. 1995. *Planting the Future*. Ames: Iowa State University Press.

Block, Fred. 1990. *Postindustrial Possibilities*. Berkeley: University of California Press.

Bluestone, Barry, and Bennett Harrison. 1982. *The Deindustrialization of America*. New York: Basic Books.

Bowles, Samuel, David M. Gordon, and Thomas E. Weiskopf. 1983. *Beyond the Wasteland*. Garden City, N.Y.: Anchor Press.

Brand, Chas. J. 1914. *Marketing*. Washington, D.C.: American Farm Management Association.

Bromley, Ray. 1978. "Organization, Regulation, and Exploitation in the So-called 'Urban Informal Sector': The Street Traders of Cali, Colombia." *World Development* 6:1161–1171.

Bruno, Kenny. 1992. "The Corporate Capture of the Earth Summit." *Multinational Monitor* (July–August).

Buttel, Frederick H., Olaf F. Larson, and Gilbert W. Gillespie, Jr. 1990. *The Sociology of Agriculture*. Westport, Conn.: Greenwood Press.

Castells, Manuel, and Alejandro Portes. 1989. "World Underneath: The Origins, Dynamics, and Effects of the Informal Economy." Pp. 11–37 in A. Portes, M. Castells, and L. Benton, eds., *The Informal Economy*. Baltimore: Johns Hopkins University Press.

Center for Rural Affairs. 1988. "Agriculture: A Foundation for Rural Economic Development." *Center for Rural Affairs Newsletter*, November SR-5–SR-8.

Cochrane, Willard W. 1958. *Farm Prices: Myths and Reality*. Minneapolis: University of Minnesota Press.

Cone, Cynthia A., A. Myhre, and M. A. Grey. 2000. "Community-Supported Agriculture: A Sustainable Alternative to Industrial Agriculture?" *Human Organization* 59:187–197.

Cone, Cynthia, and Ann Kakaliouras. 1995. "The Quest for Purity, Stewardship of the Land, and Nostalgia for Socialability: Resocializing Commodities through Community Supported Agriculture." CSA Farm Network, 130 Ruckytucks Road, Stillwater, NY 12170 (self-published).

DeLind, Laura B. 2002. "Place, Work, and Civic Agriculture: Fields for Cultivation." *Agriculture and Human Values* 19:217–224.

Domhoff, G. William. 1983. *Who Rules America Now? A View for the '80s*. Englewood Cliffs, N.J.: Prentice Hall.

Drabenstott, Mark. 1999. "New Futures for Rural America: The Role for Land-Grant Universities." William Henry Hatch Memorial Lecture, presented to the Annual Meeting of the National Association of State Universities and Land-Grant Colleges. San Francisco (November 8).

Dyck, Bruno. 1992. "Inside the Food System: How Do Community Supported Farms Work?" *Marketing Digest* (August).

Esman, Milton J., and Norman T. Uphoff. 1984. *Local Organizations: Intermediaries in Rural Development*. Ithaca, N.Y.: Cornell University Press.

Evenson, R. E., V. Santaniello, and D. Zilberman. 2002. *Economic and Social Issues in Agricultural Biotechnology*. Wallingford, N.Y.: CABI.

Ferguson, Sarah. 1999. "A Brief History of Grassroots Greening in NYC." In *Avanat Gardening: Ecological Struggle in the City and the World*. Brooklyn, N.Y.: Autonomedia.

Fieldhouse, Paul. 1996. "Community Shared Agriculture." *Agriculture and Human Values* 13 (3): 43–47.

Fisher, James R., and James J. Zuiches. 1994. "Challenges Confronting Agricultural Research at Land Grant Universities." Issue paper 5. Council for Agricultural Science and Technology, Ames, Iowa. http://www.cast-science.org/chal_ip.htm.

Fitzgerald, Deborah. 2003. *Every Farm a Factory: The Industrial Ideal in American Agriculture*. New Haven, Conn.: Yale University Press.

Flora, Cornelia B. 1995. "Social Capital and Sustainability: Agriculture and Communities in the Great Plains and the Corn Belt." *Research in Rural Sociology and Development* 6:227–246.

Flora, Jan L., Jeff Sharp, Cornelia B. Flora, and B. Newlon. 1997. "Entrepreneurial Social Infrastructure and Locally Initiated Economic Development." *Sociological Quarterly* 38:623–645.

Friedland, William. 1994. "The New Globalization: The Case of Fresh Produce." Pp. 210–231 in Alessandro Bonanno et al., eds., *From Columbus to Conagra: The Globalization of Agriculture and Food*. Lawrence: University of Kansas Press.

Frydenlund, John E. 2002. "The Erosion of Freedom to Farm." Background paper 1523. Washington, D.C.: The Heritage Foundation.

Gardner, Bruce. 2002. *American Agriculture in the Twentieth Century: How It Flourished and What It Cost*. Cambridge, Mass.: Harvard University Press.

Gatlin, Greg. 1999. "Frito-Lay Shuts Down Marlboro Plant." *Boston Herald*, January 27, p. 31.

Gilbert, Jess, and Raymond Akor. 1988. "Increasing Structural Divergence in U.S. Dairying: California and Wisconsin since 1950." *Rural Sociology* 53:56–72.

Goldschmidt, W. 1946. *Small Business and the Community.* Report of the Smaller War Plants Corporation to the Special Committee to Study Problems of American Small Business. Washington, D.C.: U.S. Government Printing Office.

———. 1978. *As You Sow.* Montclair, N.J.: Allanheld, Osmun.

Goodman David, and E. Melanie DuPuis. 2002. "Knowing Food and Growing Food: Beyond the Production-Consumption Debate in the Sociology of Agriculture." *Sociologia Ruralis* 42:5–22.

Gould, Joseph E. 1961. *The Chautauqua Movement: An Episode in the Continuing American Revolution.* New York: State University of New York.

Green, Joanna, and Duncan Hilchey. 2002. *Growing Home: A Guide to Reconnecting Agriculture, Food and Communities.* Ithaca, N.Y., Community, Food, and Agriculture Program, Department of Development Sociology, Cornell University.

Greer, Lane. 1999. *Community Supported Agriculture.* Business Management Series. Fayetteville, Ark.: ATTRA. http:///www.attra.org/attra-pub/csa.html.

Gussow, Joan D. 1991. *Chicken Little, Tomato Sauce, and Agriculture: Who Will Produce Tomorrow's Food?* New York: Bootstrap Press.

Hamm, Michael W. 1993. "The Potential for a Localized Food Supply in New Jersey." Paper presented at the Environment, Culture, and Food Equity Conference. Penn State University (June).

Harper, Douglas A. 2001. *Changing Works: Visions of a Lost Agriculture.* Chicago: University of Chicago Press.

Hart, Philip. 1992. "Marketing Agricultural Produce." Pp. 162–206 in I. R. Bowler, ed., *The Geography of Agriculture in Developed Market Economies.* New York: John Wiley and Sons.

Heady, Earl. 1976. "The Agriculture of the U.S." *Scientific American* 235:107–127.

Hedden, Walter P. 1929. *How Great Cities Are Fed.* New York: D. C. Heath and Co.

Heffernan, William D. 1999. *Consolidation in the Food and Agriculture System.* Report to the National Farmers Union. http://nfu.org/.

Hemlick, Ralph. 1991. "Agriculture Adapts to Urbanization: Linking Agriculture to the Economy." *Food Review* (U.S. Department of Agriculture) 14 (1): 21.

Hilchey, Duncan, Thomas A. Lyson, and Gilbert W. Gillespie. 1995. *Farmers' Markets and Rural Economic Development.* Community Agriculture Development Series. Ithaca, N.Y.: Cornell University, Farming Alternatives Program, Department of Rural Sociology.

Hill, Stephen. 1995. "The Social Organization of Boards of Directors." *British Journal of Sociology* 46:245–278.

Hinrichs, C. Clare. 2003. "The Practice and Politics of Food System Localization." *Journal of Rural Studies* 19:33–45.

Hinrichs, C. Clare, and Rick Welsh. 2003. "The Effects of the Industrialization of U.S. Livestock Agriculture on Promoting Sustainable Production Practices." *Agriculture and Human Values* 20:125–141.

Hughes, Megan E., and Richard H. Mattson. 1992. *Farmers' Markets in Kansas: A Profile of Vendors and Market Organization.* Report of Progress 658. Manhattan, Kans.: Experiment Station, Kansas State University.

Ingelhart, Ronald. 1997. *Modernization and Postmodernization: Cultural, Economic, and Political Change in 43 Societies.* Princeton, N.J.: Princeton University Press.

Inkeles, Alex. 1966. *The Modernization of Man.* Cambridge, Mass.: The Center for International Affairs, Harvard University.

Irwin, Michael, Charles Tolbert, and Thomas Lyson. 1997. "How to Build Strong Towns." *American Demographics* 19 (2): 42–47.

Jeffers, H. W. 1916. *How the Investigator in Farm Management Problems Can Help the Farmer.* Washington, D.C.: American Farm Management Association.

Jensen, Leif, Gretchen T. Cornwell, and Jill Findeis. 1995. "Informal Work in Nonmetropolitan Pennsylvania." *Rural Sociology* 60: 91–107.

Johnston, Thomas, and Christopher Bryant. 1987. "Agricultural Adaptation: The Prospects for Sustaining Agriculture Near Cities." Pp. 9–21 in William Lockeretz, ed., *Sustaining Agriculture Near Cities.* Ankeny, Iowa: Soil and Water Conservation Society.

Kadlec, J. E. 1985. *Farm Management: Decisions, Operation, Control.* Englewood Cliffs, N.J.: Prentice Hall.

Kaufman, Philip R. 2000. "Consolidation in Food Retailing: Prospects for Consumers and Grocery Suppliers."*Agricultural Outlook* (Economic Research Service, USDA) (August).

———. 2000. "Grocery Retailers Demonstrate Urge to Merge." *Food Review* (May–August): 29–34.

Kay, Ronald D. 1986. *Farm Management: Planning, Control, and Implementation*. New York: McGraw-Hill.

Kittredge, J. 1996. "Community Supported Agriculture: Rediscovering Community," Pp. 253–260 in W. Vitek and W. Jackson, eds., *Rooted in the Land: Essays on Community and Place*. New Haven, Conn.: Yale University Press.

Kloppenburg, Jack J. 1991. "Social Theory and the De/reconstruction of Agricultural Science: Local Knowledge for an Alternative Agriculture." *Rural Sociology* 56:519–548.

Kloppenburg, Jack, J. Hendrickson, and G. W. Stevenson. 1996. "Coming into the Foodshed." *Agriculture and Human Values* 13: 33–42.

Kneen, Brewster. 1993. *From Land to Mouth: Understanding the Food System*. Toronto: NC Press.

Kolb, J. H., and Edmund de S. Brunner. 1940. *A Study of Rural Society: Its Organization and Changes*. Boston: Houghton Mifflin Co.

Korten, David C. 1995. *When Corporations Rule the World*. West Hartford, Conn.: Kumarian Press.

Kramer, Mark. 1987. *Three Farms*. Cambridge, Mass.: Harvard University Press.

Krebs, A. V. 1992. *The Corporate Reapers*. Washington, D.C.: Essential Books.

Krimsky, Sheldon, and Roger P. Wrubel. 1996. *Agricultural Biotechnology and the Environment: Science, Policy, and Social Issues*. Urbana: University of Illinois Press.

Lehman, Karen, and Al Krebs. 1996. "Control of the World's Food Supply." Pp. 123–130 in J. Mander and E. Goldsmith, eds., *The Case against the Global Economy*. San Francisco: Sierra Club Books.

Lobao, Linda. 1990. *Locality and Inequality*. Albany, N.Y.: SUNY-Albany Press.

Lyson, Thomas A. 1999. "From Plow to Plate: The Transformation of New York's Food and Agricultural System since 1910." Pp. 157–168 in T. A. Hirschl and T. B. Heaton, eds., *New York in the 21st Century*. Greenwich, Conn.: Greenwood Press.

Lyson, Thomas A. 2000. "Moving toward Civic Agriculture." *Choices* (third quarter): 42–45.

Lyson, Thomas A., and Charles C. Geisler. 1992. "Toward a Second Agricultural Divide: The Restructuring of American Agriculture." *Sociologia Ruralis* 32:248–263.

Lyson, Thomas A., Charles C. Geisler, and Charles Schlough. 1998. "Preserving Community Agriculture in a Global Economy." Pp. 181–216 in R. K. Olson and T. A. Lyson, eds., *Under the Blade: The Conversion of Agricultural Landscapes*. Lincoln: University of Nebraska Press.

Lyson, Thomas A., Gilbert Gillespie, and Duncan Hilchey. 1995. "Farmers' Markets and the Local Community: Bridging the Formal and Informal Economy." *American Journal of Alternative Agriculture* 10:108–113.

Lyson, Thomas A., and Judy Green. 1999. "The Agricultural Marketscape: A Framework for Sustaining Agriculture and Communities in the Northeast." *Journal of Sustainable Agriculture* 15 (2/3): 133–150.

Lyson, Thomas A., and Annalisa L. Raymer. 2000. "Stalking the Wily Multinational: Power and Control in the U.S. Food System." *Agriculture and Human Values* 17:199–208.

Lyson, Thomas A., and Charles M. Tolbert. 1996. "Small Manufacturing and Nonmetropolitan Socioeconomic Well-Being." *Environment and Planning-A* 28:1779–1794.

MacKenzie, Lynn Ryan. 1994. "Capitalism, Power, and Community Well-Being : Developing a Model for Understanding the Effect of Local Economic Configuration on Cities and Their Citizens." Ph.D. dissertation, Cornell University.

Mander, Jerry, and Edward Goldsmith. 1996. *The Case against the Global Economy*. San Francisco: Sierra Club Books.

Mann, S. A., and J. M. Dickinson. 1978. "Obstacles to the Development of a Capitalist Agriculture." *The Journal of Peasant Studies* 5:466–481.

McMichael, Philip. 1996. *Development and Social Change*. Thousand Oaks, Calif.: Pine Forge Press.

Mehta, Kala. 2000. *Findings from the National Agricultural Workers Survey (NAWS) 1997-1998: A Demographic and Employment Profile of United States Farmworkers*. Washington, D.C.: U.S. Department of Labor.

Merrill, Richard. 1971. "Toward a Self-Sustaining Agriculture." Pp. 284-327 in R. Merrill, ed., *Radical Agriculture*. New York: Harper Colophon Books.

Mills, C. Wright. 1951. *White Collar: The American Middle Classes*. New York: Oxford University Press.

———. 1956. *The Power Elite*. New York: Oxford University Press.

———. 1964. *Sociology and Pragmatism: The Higher Learning in America*. New York: Paine-Whitman Publishers.

Mills, C. Wright, and Melville Ulmer. 1946. *Small Business and Civic Welfare*. Report of the Smaller War Plants Corporation to the Special Committee to Study Problems of American Small Business. Document 135. U.S. Senate, 79th Congress, 2nd session, February 13. Washington, D.C.: U.S. Government Printing Office.

Mooney, Patrick H. 1982. "Labor Time, Production Time, and Capitalist Development in Agriculture: A Reconsideration of the Mann-Dickinson Thesis." *Sociologia Ruralis* 22:279-291.

Moser, Collette. 1978. "Informal Sector or Petty Commodity Production: Dualism or Dependence in Urban Development." *World Development* 6:1041-1064.

Munton, Richard. 1992. "Factors of Production in Modern Agriculture." Pp. 56-84 in Ian R. Bowler, ed., *The Geography of Agriculture in Developed Market Economies*. New York: John Wiley and Sons.

National Association of State Universities and Land-Grant Colleges. 1995. *The Land-Grant Tradition*. Washington, D.C.: National Association of State Universities and Land-Grant Colleges.

Nevins, Alan. 1962. *The Origins of the Land-Grant Colleges and State Universities: A Brief Account of the Morrill Act of 1862 and Its Results*. Washington, D.C.: Civil War Centennial Commission.

Norberg-Hodge, Helena, Todd Merrifield, and Steven Gorelick. 2000. "Bringing the Food Economy Home." International Society for Ecology and Culture, Berkeley, Calif. www.isec.org.uk.

Northeast Dairy Business. 1999. "Market Gorilla." *Northeast Dairy Business* 1 (6): 11.

Pahl, R. E., and Clare Wallace. 1985. "Household Work Strategies in Economic Recession." Pp. 189–227 in N. Redclift and E. Mingione, eds., *Beyond Employment*. Oxford: Basil Blackwell.

Patch, Elizabeth P. 1995. *Plant Closings and Employment Loss in Manufacturing*. New York: Garland.

Pepsico. 2003. *2003 Pepsico Annual Report, Pepsico Factbook*. http://www.pepsico.com.

Perrow, Charles. 1993. "Small Firm Networks." Pp. 377–492 in R. Swedberg, ed., *Explorations in Economic Sociology*. New York: Russell Sage Foundation.

Piore, Michael J., and Charles F. Sabel. 1984. *The Second Industrial Divide*. New York: Basic Books.

Polanyi, Karl. 1944. *The Great Transformation*. New York: Farrar and Rinehart.

Putnam, Robert M. 1993. *Making Democracy Work*. Princeton, N.J.: Princeton University Press.

Rees, William E. 1997. "Why Urban Agriculture?" *Urban Agriculture Notes*. http://www.cityfarmer.org/rees.html.

Rhodus, Tim, Janet Schwartz, and James Hoskins. 1994. *Ohio Consumer Opinions of Roadside Markets and Farmers' Markets*. Columbus, Ohio: Department of Horticulture, Ohio State University.

Riedl, Brian. 2002. *Still at the Federal Trough: Farm Subsidies for the Rich and Famous Shattered Records in 2001*. Background paper 1542. Washington, D.C.: The Heritage Foundation.

Ritchie, Mark. 1993. "NAFTA's Grim Harvest, Free Trade and Sustainable Agriculture." *Multinational Monitor* 14 (5).

Robinson, Robert V., and Carl M. Briggs. 1991. "The Rise of Factories in Nineteenth-Century Indianapolis." *American Journal of Sociology* 97:622–656.

Rostow, W. W. 1975. *How It All Began: Origins of the Modern Economy*. New York: McGraw-Hill.

Rural Advancement Foundation International. 1999. "The Gene Giants: Masters of the Universe." http://www.etcgroup.org/.

Sabel, Charles F. 1993. "Studied Trust: Building New Forms of Cooperation in a Volatile Economy." Pp. 104–144 in R. Swedberg, ed., *Explorations in Economic Sociology*. New York: Russell Sage Foundation.

Sassen-Koob, Saskia. 1989. "New York City's Informal Economy." Pp. 60–77 in A. Portes, M. Castells, and L. Benton, eds., *The Informal Economy*. Baltimore: Johns Hopkins University Press.

Schlosser, Eric. 2001. *Fast Food Nation*. Boston: Houghton Mifflin.

Schwartz, Dona. 1992. *Waucoma Twilight: Generations of the Farm*. Washington, D.C.: Smithsonian Institution Press.

Shelton, Anthony. 2002. *Agricultural Biotechnology: Informing the Dialogue*. Ithaca, N.Y.: Cornell University, College of Agriculture and Life Sciences.

Shuman, Michael H. 1998. *Going Local: Creating Self-reliant Communities in a Global Age*. New York: Free Press.

Smith, Stew. 1992. "'Farming'—It's Declining in the U.S." *Choices* 7 (1): 8–10.

Sommers, Larry. 1984. *The Community Garden Book: New Directions for Creating and Managing Neighborhood Food Gardens in Your Town*. Burlington, Vt.: National Association for Gardening.

Sonberg, Lynn. 1995. *The Health and Nutrient Bible*. New York: Simon and Schuster.

Stoll, Steven. 1998. *The Fruits of Natural Advantage: Making the Industrial Countryside in California*. Berkeley: University of California Press.

Taylor, Lee, and Arthur R. Jones, Jr. 1964. *Rural Life and Urbanized Society*. New York: Oxford University Press.

Tickamyer, Ann R., and Teresa A. Wood. 1998. "Identifying Participation in the Informal Economy Using Survey Research Methods." *Rural Sociology* 63: 323–348.

Tocqueville, Alexis de. 1836. *Democracy in America*. London: Saunders and Otley.

Tolbert, Charles M., Thomas A. Lyson, and Michael Irwin. 1998. "Local Capitalism, Civic Engagement, and Socioeconomic Well-being." *Social Forces* 77:401–428.

United States Census Office. 1872. *A Compendium of the Ninth Census.* Washington, D.C.: U.S. Government Printing Office.

Warren, George F. 1914. *Farm Management.* New York: MacMillan Co.

Waters, Alice. 1990. "The Farm-Restaurant Connection." Pp. 113–124 in Robert Clark, ed., *Our Sustainable Table.* San Francisco: North Point Press.

Welsh, Rick. 1996. *The Industrial Reorganization of U.S. Agriculture.* Policy Studies Report No. 6. Greenbelt, Md.: Henry A. Wallace Institute for Alternative Agriculture.

————. 1997. "Vertical Coordination, Producer Response, and the Locus of Control over Agricultural Production Decisions." *Rural Sociology* 62:491–507.

————. 2003. "Agro-food System Restructuring and the Geographic Concentration of U.S. Swine Production." *Environment and Planning-A* 35:215–229.

Wentz, Laurel. 1992. "How Martin Sees Grand Met's Global Role." *Advertising Age* 63 (17): 11,14.

Whyte, William H. 1956. *The Organization Man.* New York: Simon and Schuster.

Wilkins, Jennifer L. 1995. "Seasonal and Local Diets: Consumers' Role in Achieving a Sustainable Food System." Pp. 149–166 in H. K. Schwarzweller and T. A. Lyson, eds., *Research in Rural Sociology and Development: Sustainable Agriculture and Rural Communities,* vol. 6. Greenwich, Conn.: Jai Press.

Woodsworth, Alexandra. 1995. "Community Gardening: A Vancouver Perspective." *Urban Agriculture Notes.* http://www.cityfarmer.org/Woodsworth.html.

Yes! 1997. "Top Trends '97." *Yes! A Journal of Positive Futures* (spring).

Young, Frank W. 1999. *Small Towns in Multilevel Society.* New York: University Press of America.

Zeitlin, Jonathon. 1989. "Introduction." *Economy and Society* 18: 367–373.

INDEX

Agribusiness firms: boards of directors, 54–57; and consumer choice, 57; and farmers, 58; and technological treadmill, 18

Agricultural development, models of, 70–78

Agricultural districts, 87

Agricultural economics, 23

Agricultural economists, 17, 22

Agricultural labor. *See* Farm labor

Agricultural literacy, 26, 62

Agricultural regionalization, 3

Agricultural treadmill. *See* Technological treadmill

Agriculture: biotechnology revolution, 20–21; in California, 5, 38; chemical revolution, 19–20; industrial model, 2; mechanical revolution, 19; in New York, 5; in Northeast, 6. *See also* Farming

Albrecht, Don, 43

American Farm management Association, 17–18

"American Way of Farming," 21

Barber, Benjamin, 77

Beus, Curtis, 79

Block, Fred, 72

Bluestone, Barry, 82

Brand, Charles, 18

Briggs, Carl, 14

Brunner, Edmund de S., 9

Chautauquas, 15, 108n

City farming. *See* Urban agriculture

Civic agriculture: and agricultural literacy, 62, 101–102; as antithesis of commodity agriculture, 73; characteristics of, 85–87; and civic community, 105; and community development, 98, 105; and community problem solving, 77; and consumer demand, 61, 81; definition of, 1–2; and democracy, 76–77; and ecological biology, 75; and economic development, 84; and economic embeddedness, 62, 101; and the environment, 74; and equity, 74; and factory farms, 62; as ideal type, 117n; measurement of, 97–98; and networks of producers, 63; in New York State, 97–98; in the Northeast, 84; policies to support, 104; and social movements, 78, 104; and sustainable agriculture, 79–81, 102; theoretical foundations, 64–78

Civic community, 69–70, 73, 75–76, 105

Civic economy, 25–29

Civic engagement, 69, 103

Civic enterprises, 65

Civic farmers, 62

Civic spirit, 65

Civil society, 69

Cochrane, Willard, 19

Commodity agriculture: and agricultural policy, 100; and animal science, 100; government subsidies, 100–101; and land grant universities, 99–100; and plant science, 100; and production contracts, 100. *See also* Factory farms; Industrial agriculture

Communities, early rural, 8

SDSU

Library of Congress Cataloging-in-Publication Data

Lyson, Thomas A.
Civic agriculture : reconnecting farm, food, and community /
Thomas A. Lyson.
    p.   cm.— (Civil society)
Includes bibliographical references and index.
ISBN 1–58465–413–9 (cloth : alk. paper) — ISBN 1–58465–414–7
(pbk. : alk. paper)
    1. Agriculture—Economic aspects—United States.
2. Agriculture—Social aspects—United States. 3. Agriculture,
Cooperative—United States. 4. Community development—
United States. I. Title. II. Series.
HD1761.L97 2004
338.1'0973—dc22   2004005364